Looking Glass Shattered
Questions and Answers that Heal Old Wounds

By

My Human Compassion

Websites:

www.mhc333.com
www.myhumancompassion.com
www.humancivilrights.com
www.streevy.com
www.astringofwords.com
www.pokethedog.net

Email:

contact@myhumancompassion.com

Word Count: 51,827

Looking Glass Shattered

Names and locations were changed to promote first nation-healing.

Looking Glass Shattered (LGS) is the first of a series of writings initiating my unique transcending journeys. The following picture is one of many heroes I met on my journey.

**The now of my well-being guides my actions and results.
I own my actions and results.**

Note: Disregard older versions of the diary you might have received as I hiked across the country. My older words spoke from fear. These words speak from compassion. This is my first diary completed on 3/13/2013. This date holds our compassion-based numbers of 3 and 333. My future travels will reveal much more about the meanings of 3 and 333. This book/diary is a platform for my bid to be the president of the USA in 2016.

LGS Paperback: http://www.amazon.com/dp/0615666752

Contents

Dedication

I dedicate my words to liberty, equality, justice, freedom, and compassion. We live in difficult times. These principles have become fuzzy in the hands of humanity.

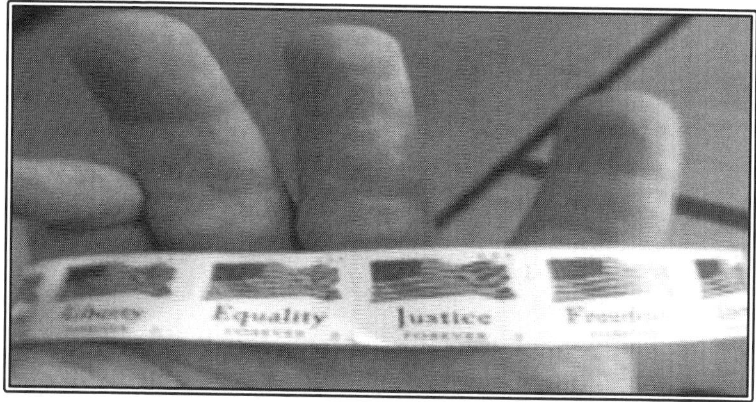

I am lead by these ideals so they become forever engraved in stone.

Compassion is my human ability to understand the well-being of others and myself. This is my desire to relieve suffering. I learn why others act the way they do. I own my human compassion to help relieve the sufferings of others. Owning compassion is how I heal.

Preface

I have devoted my time and money to help others heal from illness and trauma. It is through these actions I gain my inner-self name of My Human Compassion and it's acronym MHC.

I present the following writings in the form of a diary. This is how I heal old wounds. These are my true records of what happened over the course of my life. My diary confirms my thoughts and ideas over the last forty-five years. This diary will evolve into a workshop.

The words first nation refers to every human who has ever been born and will be born. We are all indigenous people to somewhere on this planet. Everyone is a loved member of our tribal first nation called humanity.

Everything and everyone is composed of transcending light vibrations - all living and non-living things. This is also referred to as the divine. Everyone is a part of all oneness folding into past, present, future, known, and unknown.

A transcending light quest is a first nation-healing ceremony. I left my home to spend unspecified days and nights traveling. I was determined to heal my old wounds. I gained new attachments with transcending light vibrations.

I was tired of my fourteen-year career in technology so I sold all my possessions and I put the bare minimum items of clothing and toiletries into what I call a transcending light quest backpack. It was April 2011 and I set off to explore the country.

I worked on the foundations to this diary in 2010. I needed this quest to complete it. I learned golden insights into love, compassion, and healing. This is my turning point in life to own evolutionary views on transcending. Transcending came to me while meeting new people, exploring new places, and owning personal transformation. A locate sign on the streets of Atlanta, Georgia symbolizes my brand new approach to living.

My life has involved healing. I helped develop the infrastructure and raised thousands to support a halfway house in Knoxville Tennessee. My Mom started this rehabilitation center in the 1970s. Their mission educates others on how to overcome addictions.

I gave my time and money to a charity that helps heal homeless children in Atlanta, Georgia. I lead the creation of a dinner and raised money to give presents to children who had never celebrated Christmas. My human compassion sprung forth to give them what they never had. They got every present on their wish list.

I have worked at homeless and domestic abuse shelters. I love to help teach others on how to attain a happy success filled life. I share my writings of inspiration and hope.

I donated hundreds to help support a foundation in Portland Oregon that creates new charities. I donated clothes to help hurricane Irene victims in Vermont. I love to help Veterans.

I became disappointed with popular therapy, self-help, and charity. Many charities are not donating the time and money, as I know they can. Popular therapy and self-help can prevent healing. This is why I created this diary. This diary has the healing I need.

The healing power of the number three exists in every culture. Energy, matter, and light are three essentials making up all living and non-living things. Our planet earth is the 3rd planet from the sun. Everything evolves from three and every one is attached to three.

AUM and its symbol 🕉 remind me of constant continual change. This is what everyone and everything must go through. AUM holds all known and unknown matter, energy, and light. It vibrates throughout the body and penetrates every soul.

The number three has led my life. My childhood address and a relative's phone number have 8333. The totals on my bills often contain 3 or 333. I check the time and it usually has a 3, 33, or 333. This is a 333 New York City address I visited on my quest.

The ॐ AUM symbol looks like 3. I use the number three to equal AUM. Healing energies of 3, 333, and AUM are in everyone and everything. My diaries arc founded on carefully selected 3-based words, 3-guided chapter headings, and a $13.33 price. We can become a Transcended Champion through the spiritual power of 3.

The pineal gland or 3rd eye is inside the forehead. This is where my personal transformations take place. My 3 equals ॐ spiritual transcending happens here.

Friends and family called me by different birth names. Each chapter coincides with my birth names as I transcend through life. I went by Danny from birth to fifteen. My Danny time represents inner-self child years. I went by Dan from fifteen to twenty-one. Dan is my inner-self adult period. I went by Daniel from twenty-one into my forties. Daniel is my inner-self parent age.

I include twelve first nation-healing names corresponding with my progressions from birth into my forties. These are inner-self names I aspire to own. My inner-self child owns inner-self playful, voice now heard, and inner-self love. My inner-self adult owns inner-self woman, inner-self man, inner-self forgiven, others-self forgiven, and my human compassion. My inner-self parent owns inner-self protected, voice now validated, compassion-based parent, and inner-self transcending.

My inner-self child owns play, laughter, and trust so I may overcome life hardships. My inner-self adult reminds me to work hard so I can get my needs met. My inner-self parent teaches me positive core values and protects me.

Danny-Dan-Daniel, Child-Adult-Parent, Inner-Self Team, and Inner-Self Transcending symbolize all of my holistic manifestations. Inner-Self Home is where my Inner-Self Team must live.

There were many times on my transcending light quest I checked my diary into a self-publishing venue and thought I was done. I was not finished. It did not own the perfection I new it could. I had more to learn from adventures, people, and places.

Millions of years ago this planet was known as Pangaea. All continents, beings, and vegetation were joined as one. I use Pangaea to represent our earth, world, and planet. Humanity regains Pangaea through social media, our shared humanity oneness, ease of world travel, and our Age of Aquarius.

Welcome to the Age of Aquarius. Aquarius owns the love of transcending light vibrations. It is a time for freedom and guaranteed equal human civil rights for all. Everyone is becoming more charitable and more humane. My **TIP Δ** acronym represents important teachings, inspirations, and persistence.

TIP Δ - The following is my definition of needs.

I own healthy healing foods, medications, exercise, safety, acceptance, love, sleep, clothing, shelter, and a meaningful job I love.

TIP Δ – These words define the state of my current well-being.

Sight, smell, touch, taste, hearing, brain, body, blood, muscular, spinal, organs, bones, physical, awareness of my well-being, awareness of my joints/muscles in action, awareness of my balance, awareness of my body in space (lying down or jumping), and awareness of all of my inner-self chakra energy centers; tailbone, belly, solar plexus, heart, throat, 3rd eye, and top of my skull crown.

TIP Δ - This is my definition of stability.

Owning healthy maintenance of all bodily areas including brain functions, blood flow, organs, senses, moods, and transcending. All of the above go into my inner-self shopping cart.

Any Labyrinth has one twisting path leading from its beginning to its center. At the end of this path answers to any question are revealed.   I asked my life purpose at the start to this Church Labyrinth path in Phoenix, Arizona. I took this path to own my new life truths. A Labyrinth symbolizes my transcending light quest. I got to the middle and an answer came back! I am a light healer. This picture shows my aura shadow at its center ending point. The heart of a Labyrinth gave me the answer I sought.

Why am I here?
Who am I?

I gave the following adult suit and tie to a charity. Then I began hiking the Appalachian Trail (AT) to discover and own my life purpose. The AT stretches 2,100 miles from Georgia to Maine.

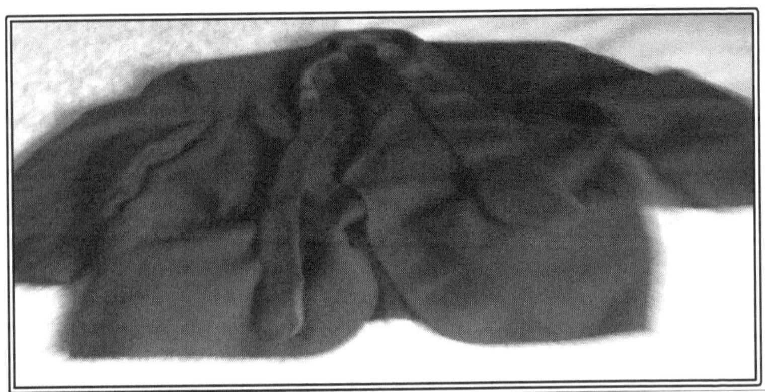

TIP Δ – At age one or one hundred anyone can own play.

The looking glass is a symbol of a mirror showing me visions of what I recognized as true. What I used to think as correct was not. I used to be an Atheist. My old outlook had my life and surroundings in fear-based crisis. I learned how to live looking glass-shattered. I had ignored the advice in my diary and I came close to death.

In the years 2011 to 201 ॐ I went on adventures in the wilderness and cities. I owned new conclusions to life truths. This is how my evolutionary questions and answers evolved. I return to the tribe of humanity to teach what I learned.

I took the following photo of myself at a loft I stayed at in Atlanta, Georgia. This is a symbol of myself being looking glass trapped inside a machine. A machine (zombie life) owns negative low vibrations of anger, shame, fear, and judgment. I learn how to shatter my looking glass zombie life.

What are life truths?
How do I heal so I can heal humanity?

I met drifters who had successful jobs and families. I found how easy it is to lose everything and everyone. I went from years of no debt into owning a lot of debt. I took a lot of risks.

Can I find my happily ever after inner-self home?
Is it safe to take a transcending light quest?

Stringing or combining words together reminds me of when I joyfully pierced fishing wire into popcorn to be strung on our family Jewish Christmas tree. Each separate kernel is lonely. When multiple kernels are combined - oh how beautiful and influential they become!

My early years of learning consisted of taking the twenty-six letters of the English language and lovingly stringing them together in brand new "creative ways". Sometimes I see words backwards or upside down. There are times when a person speaks or writes a word and I interpret it as an entirely different word. Words and their combinations have always fascinated me.

I view Pangaea through words. I am always thinking of evolutionary new letter combinations and how I may best string them together. Stringing of words demonstrates compelling new ways on educating others on how to own healed.

AStringOfWords LLC publishing company is proud to introduce the true honest beauty of our shared language. Words alone do not give them the power that 3 combinations of words convey.

It is my stringing of words together that enabled me to create a brand new self-help dictionary.

Every few months I thought I had completed this diary. I thank new people, events, and environments for helping me perfect it. This is the picture of the original cover to my diary. It read more like a technical workbook. I had strung words together such as InnerSelfTeam and ChildAdultParent. The feedback I got was combining words in this way made it too hard to read. I then separated these 3 words with spaces. My strings of words have come a "very" long way since their inception in 2010.

I am on a one-way journey to heal.
I learn to "be prepared" for my future.

Congratulations on taking the first steps to healing.
All My Best! Dan Baron - A My Human Compassion

Introduction

The plane is ascending on a gorgeous sunny day. It is early March 2011. I am south of Atlanta, Georgia looking outside a window while the ground and people grow smaller and smaller. I am anxiously awaiting my next steps. My life is in the hands of another.

I am about to embark on a life or death situation. It is either the best experience of my life or death - skydiving. I am strapped to an instructor named Tom. He is behind me like a human backpack. He decides when to open our parachute, where we land, and guides us into a safe landing. I am about to make a leap of faith.

I am wearing a t-shirt, shorts, and hiking shoes. As thousands of feet quickly disappear from sight my body fills with terror.

What am I doing? Why am I jumping out of a perfectly good airplane? Can I go back? I want to go back. I do not want to die. I want to live! Fear is a spreading cancer overwhelming my being.

I reach fifteen thousand feet and Tom says a prayer to Jesus and turns on the video camera. "What are your last words?" My mind goes blank and all I can say is "Hi Mom!"

This is all I can say in my last days of living? I am an author, comedian, and speaker and I can only muster up two words? The reason why I say two words and why I take risks is revealed later.

I had to get down on my knees, cross my arms on my chest, and knee scoot across exposed metal of the interior. It was as if I was in a deeply profound biblical moment. I am in the ethereal atmosphere looking down at a vast tiny landscape about to do a very risky act.

Upturned shards of metal rip into the flesh of my legs. I am close to the exit. The tongue of my right shoe gets stuck on an upturned piece of metal. I am doing my best to jump out of the plane but I can't. All I want to do is get out of this plane! My shoe tongue being stuck in this plane becomes symbolic of my forty something years of not knowing how to own a voice now heard.

I try to tell Tom my situation but he can't hear. The propeller sounds drown out all the other sounds. Tom realizes my situation and yells directly into my ear, "STAND UP!" I begin to stand and my shoestring and shoe tongue get cut in half. I am released from the unyielding grip of the aircraft. Thank God! I can jump now! All my fears vanish as I descend into the vastness of space.

A huge grin and pure divine love envelops my being. I am in free fall. Time stops. Adrenaline courses throughout my veins and I am gifted by glorious pleasure. What an amazing high! Blood drips from my legs but I own no pain. I am one with transcending light vibrations pure divine love. I own a dazed and blissful mood when landing in a field near the skydiving office. I understand why skydiving is so addictive.

I return to the office to take off my gear. I asked around and I am told that the airplane usually has a protecting pad at its exit. The pad on my plane had flown out of the airplane one week ago. The company had never replaced it. I still owned raw bliss as I drove off from their facility. I felt very thankful to having survived my jump. After I got home this bliss was replaced by anger.

Why was this company to cheap to buy a pad? Why didn't they tell me to wear full pants instead of shorts? Did the company purposely inflict pain upon me?

I emailed words with the owner about getting a refund. He emailed back, "No" and said, "You signed so many legal forms before this jump and my company is released from all responsibility to any injury to your body". Life is not fair.

I later learned about skydiving deaths this company had. This knowledge had me regretting my jump. I am extremely fortunate to have survived so I can write my story!

I remember positive experiences of my jump. It was a wonderful floating peace. I owned oneness with everyone and everything.

I am extremely careful about the words I use. Popular self-help words are not used. These terms go against healing and promote complexity, labels, and external influences.

I rid labels, emotion, attitude, and behavior.
I rid ill, weak, addict, and recovery.
I rid disability, handicapped, boundaries, border, and limits.
I rid assertive and disassociation.
I rid good, right, wrong, and bad.

I use transcend when referring to the words mood, emotion, movement, improve, real, reality, grow, progress, mature, advance, ethereal, ascend, spiritual, and develop.

My current state of well-being and its corresponding transcending state are my best ways to describe how I am right now.

The current state of me owning needs, losing needs, ranges of hurting or not hurting are defining my well-being transcending state.

Emotion, physical, spirituality, and attitude are brief descriptors of attempting to put into words a state of my now. The three words well-being transcending describes a long lasting now. My well-being status of now creates my moods.

I replace choice, feel, maintain, keep, and behavior with the word own. Own is long lasting and gives me responsibility for my physical, emotional, spiritual, and ethereal well-being.

Invincible, vulnerable, strong, or weak are not used. These words attach to exaggerated fantasy stories of positive super heroes defeating monsters. My diary avoids fantasy.

Assertive communication is confused with aggressive. I replace assertive with compassion-based listening and well-being availability. Popular healing words caused my healing to go out of business.

Current popular healing words own looking glass danger.

I rid disability, handicapped, or recovery. These are "old school" and harmful ways to label another. Humanity is in a brand new age of healing. Old ways of labeling are fading away.

I replace the complex term disassociation with stability or instability. I use protected for invincible and strong. I use unprotected for weak and vulnerable. I use stability and stable instead of balance or health. I use instability and unstable for imbalance or ill. I replace doctor and therapist with healer.

This art depicts our child-like ability to have a voice now heard. Everyone is free to cry, speak out, and yell if need be. Everyone owns freedom to use their voice now heard in owning their needs.

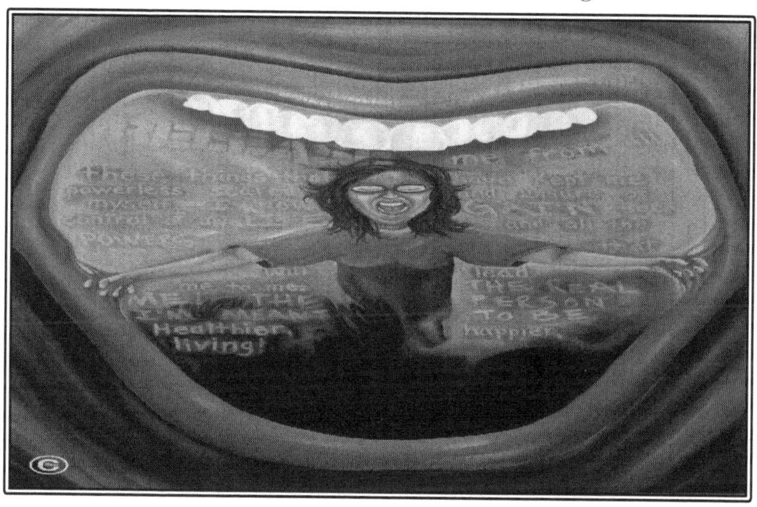

The art above is by Shamie Encinas at ShamArt44@yahoo.com. We met when I was in Phoenix, Arizona. I look deep inside any mirror to view my voice now heard and inner-self child. I transcend to be the person I must be and own a healthier way of living.

Conventional therapy taught me that running away (geographical relocation) to a new town is bad. There is the saying, "The grass is greener on the other side". I was programmed to stay in the same hometown and work on my old wounds before relocating. I realized that running away could lead to a positive reinvention of myself.

There are specific ages in any life when we must "reinvent" or face life-threatening injuries. It is my non-clinical view that cancer, car accidents, and other life threatening tragedies are occurring because a person did not reinvent when they are supposed to.

TIP Δ – Running enabled me to reinvent myself and stay alive.

TIP Δ – Every seven years each of us must reinvent ourselves.

I use set self-discipline instead of boundaries and limits. Set self-discipline allows me to say yes or no when I need to and when it matches my core values. It allows me to monitor and stabilize my well-being. This is when I own my needs and meet the needs of others through compassion-based compromise. I am well-being talking and compassion-based listening. I protect myself from abuse and defend myself from aggression.

A sensory stability hero owns societal labels of disabled, handicapped, self-harmer, recovery, addict, crazy, and mentally ill.

I used to ignore all of the daily life symbols I came across. I realized their crucial importance in the completion of my book. Signs such as this Marta train logo in Atlanta, Georgia lead me.

This book/diary is my never-give-up approach to healing. This is a must read for individuals, families, healers, veterans, and politicians. These writings are how I own the honest courageous work to heal.

I use compassion for right, good, and positive. I use anger for wrong, bad, and negative. I pop the balloon of pop culture and external influences. The photo of this balloon and its shadow were taken at an Atlanta, Georgia office park where I used to work.

I jumped out of an airplane, sold all of my stuff, and started hiking the Appalachian Trails. When I started hiking I was at two hundred and thirty pounds! I had just seen a healer who wanted me to get on cholesterol medication. My ideal weight is one hundred and seventy-five pounds. I used to attach to money of jobs I hated. While working these jobs I gained a lot of weight from unhappiness. This is a photo of myself attached to the money I earned.

Liberty, justice, equality, and freedom are easily hand delivered to humanity yet My Human Compassion two-year transcending light quest through cities and wildernesses uncovered that life is not fair.

What can we do to make life fairer? Should we rid all attachments to have everything in one backpack? Could we abandon home to randomly roam the country? Why must we own womb birth guaranteed human civil rights?

Follow along with My Human Compassion who is on a desperate quest to answer these questions and give humanity the tools for healing before its collective journey heads into extinction. This is my $3 = AUM$ (universal sound vibrations telling us that everything is in constant change) evolutionary approach to heal old wounds so we can own new life foundations of success and happiness! These writings cannot be put down and its truths are impossible to forget. How is my inner-self light shining on my road to transcending?

I Never-Give-Up!

Chapter 1 Never-Give-Up!

Proud Of You!
You Own Life!
It's Not Easy
Times Seem Rough
Fall Back Now
You Are Caught
Love And Light
Peace And Joy
Alive Here Now
You're Not Alone!
Spirit And Pride!
You Have Us
Stability-Healing Heroes
Humanity And Ancestors
Transcending Light Vibrations
Compassion Is Here!
Never-Give-Up!
Never-Give-Up!
Never-Give-Up!

I brought all the wrong things on my Appalachian Trail hike. I had forgotten the Boy Scouts motto "Be Prepared". My backpack weighed more than it should and it did not fit properly. I thought it would be warm when I started my quest on April 1, 2011.

I brought three lightweight shirts, one pair of long polyester lightweight paints, and one pair of shorts. All of my clothes were made of quick dry material. The Appalachian Trail Mountains higher elevations (five thousand feet) nighttime temperatures dipped below freezing. I strung my hammock between two trees and my teeth where chattering! I had to wear every layer of clothing I owned.

I lay in my hammock while the sun was setting. What glorious transcending sights and sounds! It sounded as if millions of bees hummed together. I was in tune and owning harmonious attachment with Pangaea. I heard, smelled, touched, and visualized our shared divine vibrations.

The Appalachian Trail has many shelters made of simple wooden structures with three sides and an open front. There is a shelter about every twelve to twenty miles on the trail. At a shelter, hikers sleep like sardines - body-to-body. A shelter is enough to keep the rain and snow off. It rains a lot in the Appalachian Mountains. Everything gets wet! I lived in many shelters during my quest.

Initially, I owned a guidebook. I threw that away. I was testing to see if humanity is compassionate. Would random strangers help me? I had to ask others where water sources were. I was following the trail markers and Cairns on the 2100 mile Appalachian Trail (AT) from Georgia to Maine. The trail markers are white paint on trees. A Cairn is a stack of several stones on top of another. These stones are used when there are no trees around. This stacks of stones tells me which way to hike. The entire AT is very well marked and it is well maintained by several hiking clubs in each state it goes through.

I hike through fields in North Carolina. My feet wore raw against my boots, which were too small for my feet. The result was aching calluses that bled. I should have brought boots two inches larger than my actual foot size due to my long hikes.

The temperature ranged from frigid cold at night into unbearable hot humidity at night. I suffered from heat dehydration. One day I was down on the ground about to drink muddy water. A kind gave me filtered water and electrolytes.

TIP Δ – I learned how to survive in the trails and cities.
TIP Δ – My ongoing life is always in a state of transcending.

Transcending is my human compassion journey of self-discovery. I learn who I am and who I must be. I challenge myself by reaching beyond my current transcending status. I maintain an available mind, question my current beliefs, and try my best to better understand others. Transcending light vibrations lead my life.

The faith of my inner-self playful child helped guide me. I recalled child-like faith during my survival in unknown cities, shelters, hospitals, and storms. My solutions are a result of honest courageous work. I illuminate and overcome challenges. I learned to love the oneness ingrained in everyone and everything. My transcending light quest taught me the key attachments I must own.

I owned and returned many different types of keys when I went from homes, hostels, hotels, shelters, and campsites. I stayed at different places for a week or months at a time.

I can never go back to the home of my childhood. My transcending light quest is my ticket to scratch off and win the prize of a stable inner-self home. The key is a symbol of how I can identify and own important attachments. This is one of many keys I owned and gave back. It matched a 33-compassion-based home I stayed at in Denver Colorado.

The theme of home echoed throughout my quest. I evolved into a resident of the universe. There are Hostels in the cities and wildernesses across Pangaea. Strangers become friends as we share the commitment of exploring the city we visit. I stayed at many wilderness and city Hostels.

Many Hostels along the AT have hiker boxes. Hikers can discard clothes they don't need and take new outfits. I hiked over a hundred miles and lost over forty pounds! I needed new smaller sized clothes that would fit properly.

I stayed at a Harpers Ferry West Virginia Hostel that is the official AT halfway point. I got a homemade shirt from a hikers box that said, "Home Team". I did some photo editing to these words. This is the picture that resulted. My old ideals of home had faded away.

I created a new home.

Through my awareness of living in AUM inner-self prayer and inner-self meditation I can own now. The three of the past, present, and future are inside AUM. In meditation when I chant AUM, I am creating sound vibrations joining my human compassion with transcending light vibrations. I can now think at a transcending light vibrational level. AUM is where my trivial affairs are lost in the desire for my new improved attachments. My AUM becomes awakened. The following equation defines my inner-self team.

3 = AUM = Inner-Self Love = Transcending Light Vibrations

Everyone is in constant continual change and this enrolls us into humanity. I own honest courageous work to own transcending. I own my transcending light vibrations of 3 = ॐ .

ॐ = Inner-Self Love
ॐ = Inner-Self Team
ॐ = Inner-Self Home

How did I survive crisis?

I show how I moved beyond crisis. I observe and stabilize my well-being to own informed actions. I am my own best healer.

ॐ = Dream Repairing Time
ॐ = Awake Transcending Time

All of my ideas are from forty-five years of living in our system. There are contradictory ideas on how to heal. Each of us has a buffet of available healing options.

Illness affects all races, gender, caste, and societies. I created this book/diary to heal old wounds and help others choose the healing, which works best for them. I discover how to heal.

The time in the womb owns transcending light vibrations of highly positive frequencies of love, compassion, peace, and enlightenment. During womb time I do not own any low negative vibrations of external influences, judgments, labels, or fears.

This is my time known as womb-healed.

Looking to add excitement to life? Trying to heal old wounds? This is the place. Follow me as my inner-self team goes on an unforgettable journey. There are many things I need to say. Creating my diary triggered deeply buried truths I was not aware of.

I am proud to have close relations with all Pangaea cultures and backgrounds. This is crucially important to my healing. I own my healing journey by recognizing I cause problem routines for myself and I learn new ways to stop them.

3 = 30 is my home for healing.

I must own purpose in every moment and transcending awareness. I allow myself to own the now in every moment. I tune into my crown, heart, and body for guidance.

Letting go of old wounds is not easy. My past is over and living there destroyed my ability to fully experience the present. I feared what was in my future so I could never enjoy my now. I must live for today so I can enjoy the love of humanity and divine healing. This is my faith that guides my unique transcending journey.

The following picture is my inner-self team owning 3 = AUM third-eye umbilical cord attachments. This attachment owns transcending light vibrations. The following picture symbolizes each of us deep down inside. This is a light worker and everyone is one. Human consciousness awakenings are sweeping across Pangaea.

This is a picture of *Looking Glass Shattered* author Dan Baron - My Human Compassion. This symbol strips away all negative vibrations. It removes looking glass illusions of overwhelming inner-self talk fears. I awaken to our divine energy flow, inner-self presence, compassion, love, and love to other selves. I rid all labels, self-created looking glass illusions of ego, and societal corruptions.

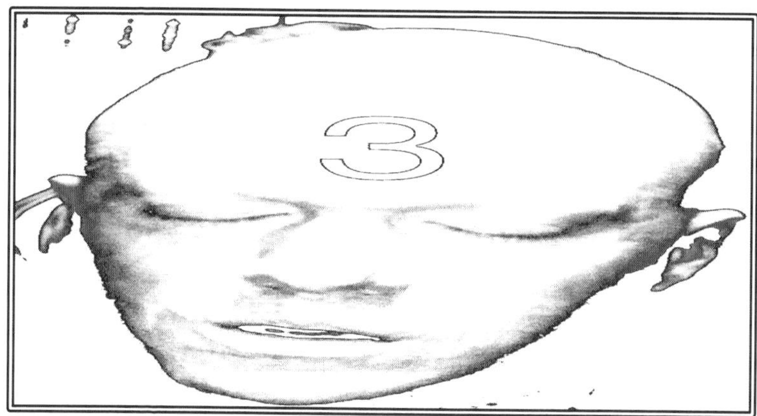

My diary questions and answers activate personalized healing. All individuals are born, raised, and exist within unique times. My time of living are different than all others. Every life suffering and healing is unique. I, nor anyone, else can ever fully understand the sufferings of another. I own compassion-based listening and well-being availability to better understand

The hand of humanity mails a package out. This is a reminder of the current fragile state of justice, equality, liberty, and freedom.

I learned new healing ideas from my quest. My changes involved a lot of honest courageous work. I completed a unique version of the 2,100-mile Appalachian Trail hike. I focused my goal to reach the top of mount Katadin Maine and I made it. I pushed my body to hike 14,000 foot high peaks in Colorado and I did that. I hiked part of the continental divide trail. I spent two years traveling from Georgia to Maine and New York City to Los Angeles.

I sold my car in 2011. This forced me to view scenery I had never noticed before. Most of the pictures in this diary were taken during my quest. I took photos of myself and I put sayings on them that I needed to manifest into reality. These included stay true and family. Many mottos in these snapshots were inspired by real tattoos of people I came across. I recommend taking photos of yourself and photo edit positive sayings onto the photo. Hang these photos over your bed or in your house so they become reality.

My pictures featured portions of street signs, placards, places, and people I met. Photographs of signs, people, and environments deeply affected me. Public transportation, walking city streets, and camping gave me unique life lessons. I lived way outside any idea of a comfort zone. I met new people and changed routines.

I report to my inner-self team main office fully aware of my problems and how I must heal. I took this photo at a construction site in Atlanta, Georgia.

How am I living my life in Pangaea?

"A lot of people may not even know they are manifesting, they are unaware. It's part of the universal attraction that we are all united with, our ancient teachers knew this. It is within us, just tap into it."

Every word, every picture, and all lives are inner-self transcending. I wear this reminder on my t-shirt.

A Mother and a Father have a ॐ = 3rd eye cord with their babies and each other. A baby has a ॐ = 3rd eye cord with parents. Humanity has a ॐ = 3rd eye cord to every human. Transcending light vibrations has a ॐ = 3rd eye cord to all.

The womb I once lived in owned all of my needs. This womb owns inner-self prayer/meditation. The womb owns no fear and it is my fresh new start. This is my 3 = ॐ symbol of womb-healed. My birth cord is cut! My Grandmother is holding me after my birth.

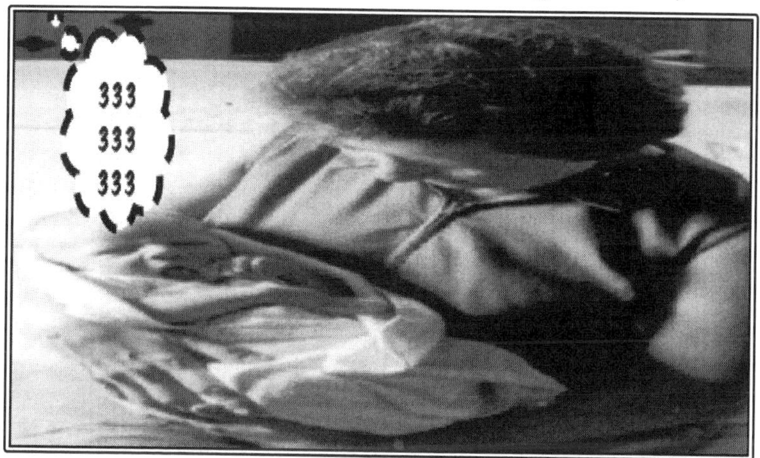

During my transcending light quest, I discovered brand new ways to heal. This involves ceremonies and objects I am in the process of creating. My healing ceremonies help humanity transcend.

I learn the positive stable 3-cord relationships I must attach with. The umbilical cord I had with my Mom was very strong. They needed a very sharp knife to cut it. Once out of the womb, I am challenged to own needs and attach with friends, family, and the tribe of humanity.

My inner-self love attaches positive umbilical cords. My inner-self protected cuts negative umbilical cords. Adding and cutting of cord relationships enrolls me into humanity.

My attempt to leave the airplane while being held back by my shoe tongue is a symbol of my desire to speak out. I learned to own my needs based on my voice. I am safe to voice my current well-being. I learn the importance of "speaking out" hurt and happiness.

Adults broke promises to me in childhood due to negative ancestry. This taught me to set low expectations for new relationships. I was yelled at in my attempt to own needs.

I am in mid-life and death is not as far away as it used to be. Death owns my humanity umbilical cord cut and a trip to a morgue. I briefly own my toe tag to become cremated and re-attach my cord to transcending light vibrations. This is a picture of my toe with a toe tag and a Hearst I came across. In the 3 of birth, life, and death I own umbilical cord attachments. Mid-life is when I worry about what my toe tag will say. Will it say I owned my true-life-purpose?

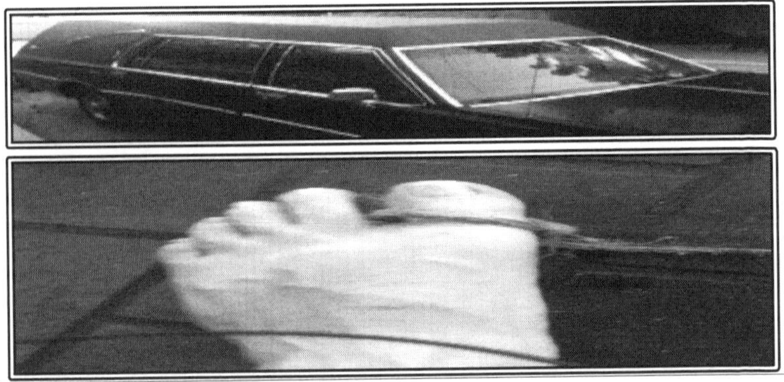

My positive core values allow me to own my needs and the needs of others based on mutual compassionate compromise. These values guide my journey to follow the signs for owning my foundations of happiness and success. I own positive core values to breathe in compassion.   Transcending light quest signs changed my life directions. This photo was taken on my Appalachian Trail hike.

This is one of many Appalachian Trail marker signs. These markers symbolize the turns every human journey has to make. Had I lost this marker, I would have owned premature death. My values, wilderness training, and transcending light vibrations saved me.

My Human Compassion needs to be remembered as having touched and healed souls. Everyone learns from there my human compassion. I seized moments with a random walk in the woods with fresh snowfall.   I owned courage in the face of adversity. I held onto friendships and an unwavering loyalty to humanity. Sometimes it takes a transcending light quest through muddy shelters, storms, and a beautiful sunset from Martha's Vineyard Massachusetts to uncover what is really waiting out there.

What is out there?

When I started my transcending light quest I had no idea what lay ahead. My passionate story burned deep inside. The story is not just about one human released into a universe. This is the life journey we all take. It is humanities 7.2 billion ups and downs. It is the laughter, the tears, the failure, and the success. It is a journey worth taking. I try, fail, and try again. Doing nothing is fear - so I try and fail with a huge grin on my face!

Where am I now?
Where do I need to be?

TIP Δ - My positive core values set my human compass.

I used to struggle with defining myself. My core values lead my human compass to own positive actions. I took this picture of my shadow inside of a street compass while walking in Denver, Colorado. This is my aura shadow representing my individual essence. My aura vibrates into our transcending light vibrations.

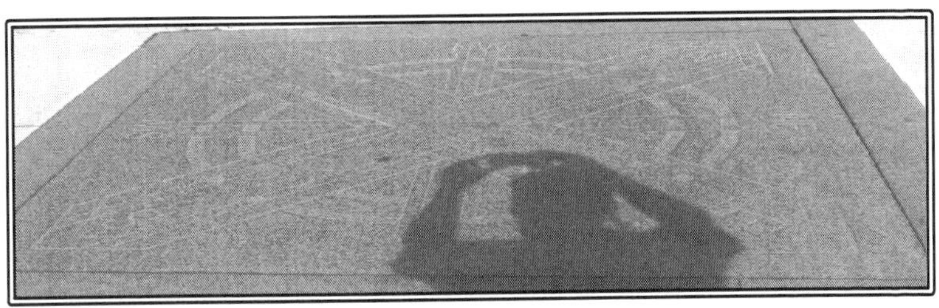

My human compass is doing no harm to another. I never steal. I never commit adultery. I obey local laws. I own my needs, safety, acceptance, and stability through mutual compassion-based compromise. I own zero prejudice to anyone.

TIP Δ - My set self-discipline guides my human compass journey.

The most important word I say is no. I say yes or no when I must say yes or no and if it agrees with my values. I walk away if saying no is not enough. I learn why I disagree with another. A person I disagree with knows why I disagree with them.

I own set self-discipline, courage, loyalty, and honesty. I balance my budget and I do not live beyond my means. I own my actions and apologize for my mistakes. I respect others, the earth, and equality. I am never afraid of change. I value culture, education, charity, trying, and failing. I fail more than I succeed and I learn the most from failing. This following is 3 days of my trying and failing.

Day 1 – I try, fail, try, fail, try, fail, and try.
Day 2 – I fail, try, fail, try, fail, try, and try.
Day 3 – I fail, fail, fail, fail, fail, fail, and fail.

Day 4 – Succeed.

TIP Δ - My inner-self survival kit owns my positive core values.

My looking glasses symbolize everything I can see. I view a blooming flower, a baby's first steps, and friends laughing.

A Phoenix bird rises from ashes to experience rebirth. On my quest across the country I had many nagging signs to visit Phoenix, Arizona. My roommate in Denver, Colorado is from Phoenix. I have friends with relatives here. I rewrote a lot of my diary after the people, places, and events in Phoenix, Arizona.

No matter the trauma, crisis, or chaos ashes I once owned I rise up from this rock bottom so I may transcend my ashes and heal.

Transcending light vibrations pick me up when I am down. I do this every single day no matter the strength of the "down pull" and no matter what may come my way.

Every human has both testosterone male hormones and estrogen female hormones. In a time after conception each of us are both male and female. My interpretation of the Chinese Yin and Yang symbol is that each of us owns equal inner-self woman and equal inner-self man. I may heal when I completely love my inner-self woman and inner-self man.

Welcome to My Human Compassion!

I am transcending out from My Human Compassion. Each of us is born to compete as we might. It seems that we always compete with someone else. How is there is a winner if there is a loser?

TIP Δ - We should make it so that everyone wins!

TIP Δ - Woman is in my Man!

TIP Δ - Man is in my Woman!

TIP Δ - Woman equals inner-self woman plus inner-self man.

TIP Δ - Man equals inner-self woman plus inner-self man.

Have you all noticed the first two letters in Woman are "Wo" and the last three letters are "Man"? Isn't this what every "Man" needs? An inner-self woman to say, "Wo!" "Slow down!"

Death on earth is not an end. Death is a shift on my unique transcending journey. The old me must die so the new me can birth into my brand new life. Every seven years in my life I have died and on the eight year I am born again. I have been overwhelmed with the sufferings of inner-self mind chatter.

Should I go to this event? Should I meet this person? Should I eat this meal? What is my future? How can I meet my needs?

We are all oneness and we are all apart of everything. Everything I see, touch, feel, hear, taste, and touch is perfection. This is the same perfection everyone owns. We are all gifted with the eternal flame of transcending light vibrations. Our oneness with the mineral, plant, and vegetable are our looking glass views into reality. We begin and end at the same place. Your journey is my journey. My transcending light quest is your expedition. Each of us owns the only label ever having any importance - Human.

TIP Δ - Every breath in and breath out is a divine gift.

Some religions practiced today do not match the teachings of "original" first-nation healing. Original first-nation Pangaea religions taught that a woman's feminine always equals a man's masculine.

The "newer" religions promote the dominance of the masculine. In many countries a woman is still considered a slave. In those places a woman cannot own the same opportunity that a man can have.

We are in desperate times where the feminine of Pangaea must rise up from the destructive ashes caused by the masculine. Rising feminine heals humanity from super storms, pollution, and war.

I love the feminine within all women and the feminine within me! I allow all feminine to transcend so I can own healed.

I took this picture in the forests of Colorado. It is transcending light vibrations - violet flame. This flame heals me when I let it in.

This symbolizes my inner-self woman ahead of my inner-self man.

This symbolizes my inner-self man ahead of my inner-self woman.

My inner-self woman and my inner-self man walk in synchronicity.

This picture is a symbol of my third-eye pineal gland. It is the AUM umbilical cord attaching the compassion of my inner-self team to my inner-self love, humanity, and our transcending light vibrations. It is the area through which my light vibrational energy resides. The third-eye is a light bulb switch activating my transcending energy. This bulb triggers while sleeping so I can reattach with our transcending light vibrations. The food I eat, relationships I have, and events I attend determine my inner-self light bulb well-being.

On light bulb   (Positive energy well-being)
Dim light bulb (Low energy well-being)
Off light bulb   (Negative energy well-being)

Positive or negative people, experiences, and ancestry either increases or decreases the transcending light vibrations of my third-eye energy. Every birth begins a unique transcending journey.

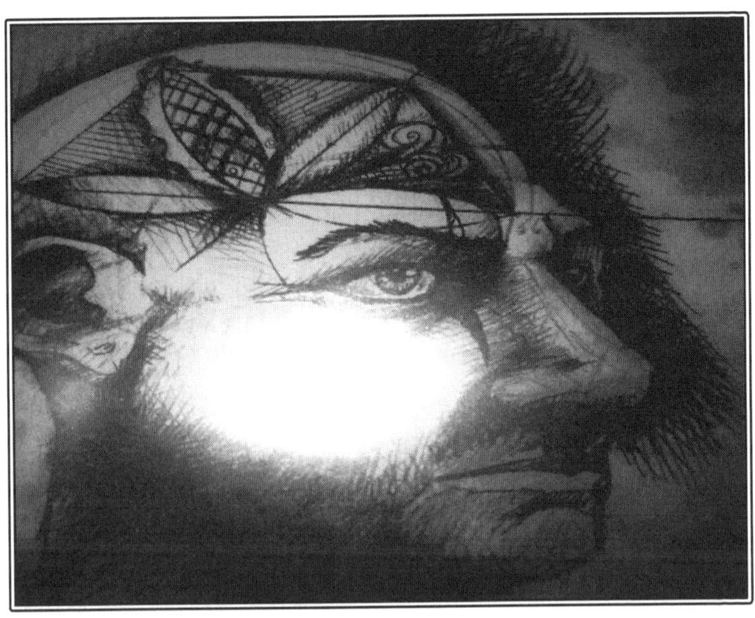

The art above is by Steven Thompson mcdurphurp@gmail.com.
His username is TranceParadox and website http://stproductions.snappages.com.

Stability-Healing Questions

How is current self-help preventing MHC from healing?

What is the MHC definition of a transcending light quest?

How are my human compass values healing MHC?

What is the MHC definition of transcending light vibrations?

How are the never-give-up approaches healing MHC?

How does working a hated job affect MHC?

Why is the key a symbol of the MHC transcending light quest?

What does inner-self home and inner-self team mean to MHC?

How does 3 = AUM heal MHC?

How can owning carefully defined self-help words help heal MHC?

How does 3, 333, and AUM help heal MHC?

What is the MHC definition of compassion?

What life direction must MHC take?

How does equal masculine and feminine heal MHC and humanity?

How does light bulb energy on, dim, and off affect MHC?

Chapter 2 Unique Transcending Journey

Matter Energy Light
3-Stimuli Feeding
Inner-Self Aware!
Illness To Healing
During Each Sleep
Negative Angry Nightmares
Compassion-Based Dreams
Sleep Owns Healing
Chaos Stability Dreamed
Leaving My Body
Reuniting Once Again
Transcending Light Vibrations

I believe. I will make a difference.
I was born with greatness!

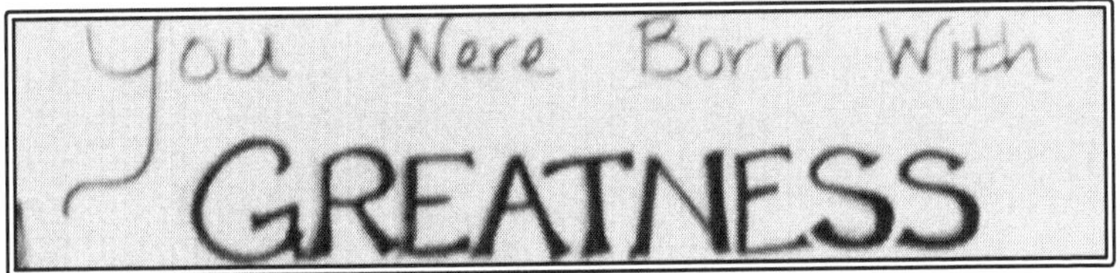

These words inspired me while owning my transcending light quest. These inspirational sayings own hope but it wasn't words keeping me safe. My free will, angels, and humanity kept me alive.

I own fond memories of late night city exploring and camping trips with new friends. I spent a month in Virginia, weeks in North Carolina, a month in Washington D.C., a month in Massachusetts, a month in Maine, weeks in Arkansas, weeks in Tennessee, a month in Austin Texas, months in New York, a month in Vermont, months in Georgia, months in Colorado, months in Arizona, weeks in Utah, a week in Nevada, and months in California.

One day on my AT hike it poured rain and there were lightening strikes everywhere. I was hiking with well-experienced outdoorsmen. I chatted with them about my goal of hiking to the next shelter.

Joe said, "If you keep going on the trail to the next shelter you place yourself at great risk. You have to hike up a tall hill and in so doing you are likely to be killed by lightening."

I smelled fear. I needed to make it up and over this hill to get to the shelter. I said, "Thank you Joe for the advice I must go on." I had to get away from fear! As I turned to go on I heard Joe say, "When you make it to the top of that hill make yourself as small as possible. This is your best chance to avoid lightening."

I slowly rose up the hill. Everything hurt and the pouring rain made each step harder. My path quickly filled with mud as volumes of water turned the trail into clumpy mud. My feet felt as if they would pop out of my boots. I pushed myself onwards and upwards. I said to myself, " I must get to that shelter."

I got to the top of the hill. I was surrounded by wonderfully healing angelic mists. Transcending light vibrations where everywhere. They cheered me to keep going when my exhaustion told me to stop. I must never-give-up! I had to make it to the sanctuary of the shelter.

When the weather is rough the inside of shelters fill up early. When I got to the shelter it was full. I had to sleep just outside the shelter entrance under the lip of the shelter roof. I had to sleep in the mud however the rain wasn't pouring on me.

I will always remember the look on the faces of other hikers. They owned the same suffering I had. I was so thankful for sleeping in the mud with worms, spiders, and snakes. The next morning the rain had cleared. Another camper and I were able to make a fire so we could dry out our clothes. This hike made me thankful for simple things. I was living in the 1800s before running water, electricity, and plumbing. This hikes made me thankful for modern conveniences. I loved hiking for weeks and held amazement whenever the trail opened up to reveal new people, places, and events.

I used to value my inner-self team based on wealth and the work I did. It is my core values making me who I am. I own positive core values in my actions and relationships. My unhappiness came from looking at external ways to define myself and resolve my problems. When I own an externally controlled life I gave up on happiness.

TIP Δ – Compassion-based values are my crucial core value.

I listen carefully to others so I can repeat back what is said. I focus on the words of others so I may understand. I don't interrupt or change the subject of those I talk with. I see if the person I talk with owns comfort or discomfort. I accept what is said. I listen to determine if this person is suffering or in trouble.

TIP Δ – I listen to others while owning high-energy love, peace, and happiness. Owning high vibrations at all times is my compassion.

TIP Δ – I never own low-energy negative vibrations others may send out. These include anger, despair, and shame. Low vibrational empathy continuously feeds negativity within me.

I refuse to get bogged down in low energies. Lowering myself to own the low vibrations of another is empathy. I spent forty years of my life owning empathy when I thought I was owning compassion.

Inner-influenced actions give me stability. This transcends me to be more successful than one hoping things get better with externally influenced pop culture, fearing, fantasy, and addictions. My inner-influenced actions transcend my compassion so I own my needs. My compassion-based values are always available.

COMPASSION

Open 7 Days

TIP Δ – Compassion is when I teach others how to own inner-self love. I heal others when they view my perpetual high-energy light bulb. I heal others and myself by owning high vibrations.

I used to conform to external societal expectations of living. I owned fearing ideas on how to live. I followed external influences of family and friends. This was my looking glass paralyzed existence.

Western and Eastern cultures govern how to dress, what types of relationships to have, how to look, and how to live. Inner-influenced action and set self-discipline protect my inner-self space.

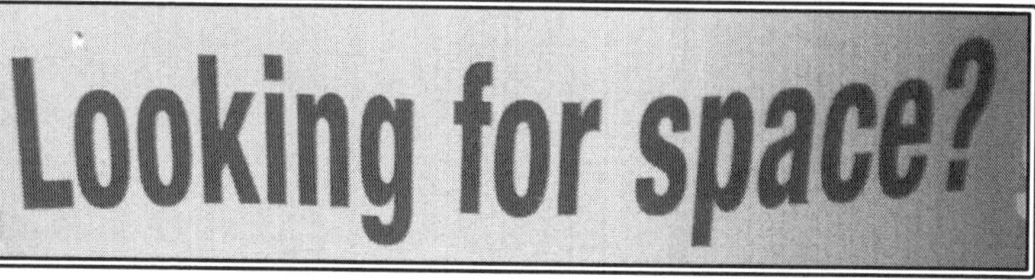

TIP Δ - I own my actions and their results.

I do not always do what others need of me. In the course of my life I must not always rely on others to pull me through. Inner-influenced actions own my success.

I avoid healers who emphasis external-influenced actions on how to heal. Healers teaching inner-influenced actions are available.

How do I own my needs?
How can I heal?

I used to ask these questions without knowing answers. My transcending light quest helped me own these answers and so much more! Are my healers helping me?

Hundreds of years ago it was kings, queens, and religious clergy who were the only ones allowed to read or write. They interpreted and told others what morality, laws, and religious doctrines said. A vast majority of people could not understand the written word.

Professionals in any role and even more so in the professions of healing and self-help who obscure explanations by using mysterious complex terminology do themselves and their roles tremendous damage. Inner-influenced healing is my personal bailout plan.

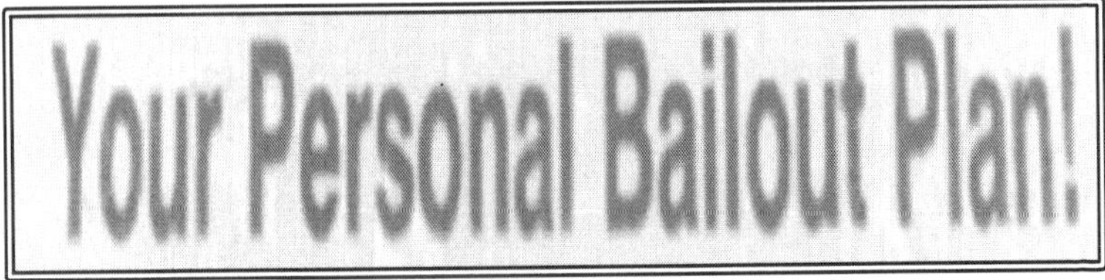

I can say no. The person I am with can say no. I can walk away from anyone and any conversation. I let others know how their actions affect me. My set self-discipline sets me free!

Set self-discipline and inner-influenced actions buys my ticket to owning liberty, equality, justice, freedom, and compassion. This photo has my shadow aura in a ticket booth at the science center in Denver, Colorado.

This photo is a set self-discipline symbol. This was taken at the New York City Museum of Art. I view this picture to own calm.

I recognize my need to privacy. I must self-discipline with others and myself. I own no responsibility to make others happy.

TIP Δ - I own a responsibility to make myself happy.

I used to fill my loneliness with low-energy partners. The word love is defined in many different ways and I used to own a love I call hyper-paradise love. This owns more love for my partner than myself. I spent years filling my life with societal ideas of a fantasy love. I gave money, intimacy, and time without set-self discipline.

Unconditional love disciplined is each partner owning each other's set self-discipline, owning each other's inner-self love, owning each other's inner-influenced actions, owning each other's core values, owning each other's compassion-based listening, and owning each other's well-being availability.

My definition of love is inner-self love and respecting myself. In turn others respect and love me. I took this photo at the Young Men's Christian Associate (YMCA) I lived at in Phoenix, Arizona.

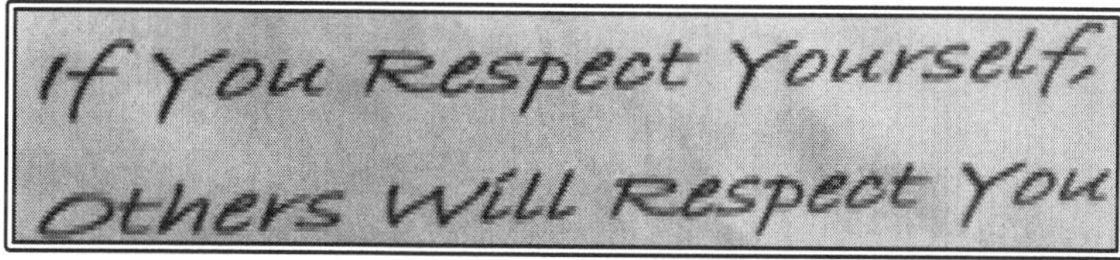

At one time, I did not respect myself and no one respected me. I had not yet learned how to own inner-self love.

My hyper-paradise love owned well-being fireworks resulting in my unnecessary suffering. Partners' compassion-based compromise owns mutual needs and we own each other's perfections/flaws.

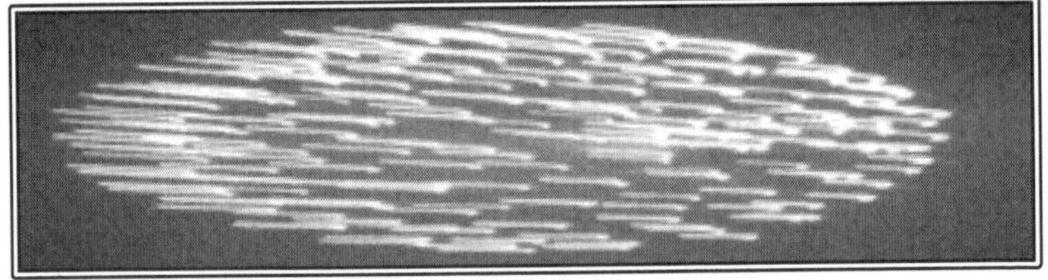

This is a picture of the engagement ring I gave to my partner Hyper-Love Forgiven after only three months. I took this action based on love instability. I owned many mistakes in this relationship. I tried to make the love of this relationship into what it could never be. I tried to sell this ring at the New York City diamond district.

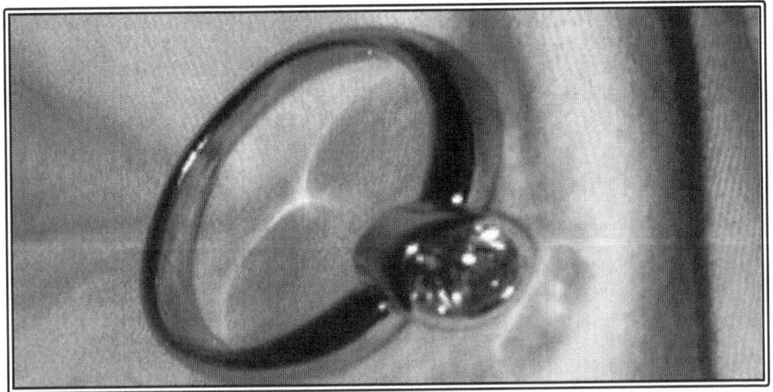

I was offered two hundred dollars when I paid close to a thousand. I refused to sell it. I felt dazed and angry as I left the store. I started walking across the street with a red light. Random strangers yelled, "Stop!" I heard this word loud and clear so I stopped in my tracks. I walked within inches of certain death. A sports car going thirty miles an hour almost killed me. It was as if lightening struck. I will always remember the shocked awakening this near death experience gave me.

There were many unusual events happening over the course of my transcending light quest. More of this is revealed in later chapters. I attempted to make something out of another, out of events, and out of experiences that can never happen. This is what defines suffering.

At one time I believed my life suffering was worse than others. My transcending light quest taught me that others have suffered far more. As I emerge from despair, my third-eye cord attaches with the suffering of humanity. This is important stability-healing hero information. I own this information to recognize universal life healing. I took this picture at a bookstore in Denver, Colorado.

TIP Δ – The following defines a stability-healing hero.

I own my flaws and I am confident in revealing them. I own my needs through my values, actions, and mutual compassion-based compromise. I set self-discipline and own stability.

Communication with stability-healing heroes gets me on the path to owning high-energy vibrations. It aids the process of making positive changes to transform my existing attitudes and heal.

Stability-healing heroes ask these questions.

How do I own stability?
How can I heal so I can help heal others?

Stability-healing hero women and men names are written in stone.

Stability-healing heroes are not strangers and not on television. These are people in my life. I talk and write about my problems so new healing opportunities transcend. Stability-healing heroes support my entry into happiness and success. This picture was taken before I took an important trip on a New York City subway.

A stability-healing hero owns the honest courageous work to heal.

TIP Δ - I became educated on new ways to heal my inner-self team.

I ask myself if my current healing improves my daily living or if I need to make changes. I create lists of what I love about the flaws, perfections, sufferings, and compassions of my stability-healing heroes. I put my three fingers together as a symbol of healing action. I say this phrase three times, "May all my healings come true".

A first nation-healing symbol is the 119-fearless hand with 3 fingers rising up. The 119-fearlessness removes 911 and all known or unknown fears. This symbol transcends my freedom.

I write down honest diary entries. I owned my old wounds far longer than I was aware of. I share my writings with stability-healing heroes. There is never any specific time limit for healing. Each person heals in the time that works best for her or him.

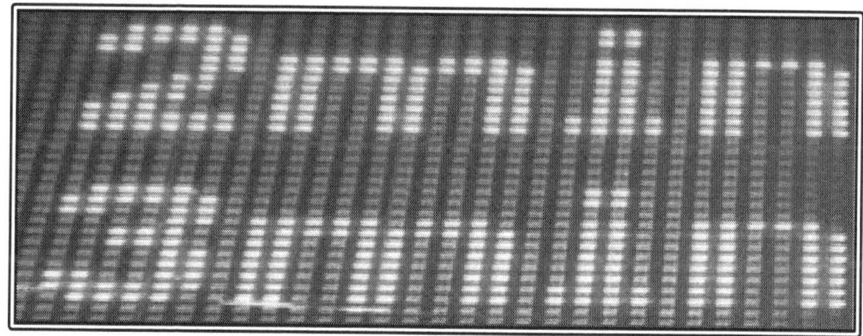

TIP Δ - I am aware of and I write down my daily healing goals.

The *Looking Glass Shattered* diary is my stability-healing diary. I write using inner-self child-like trust and playfulness. I move my unique transcending journey beyond old destructive influences. My inner-self parent holds the hand of my inner-self child. I face forward into my life with well-being availability. I took this escalator in a Marta train station located in Midtown Atlanta, Georgia.

I see a wonderfully beautiful womb-healed baby inside everyone. I see this in the eyes of a one year old and a retired person. I see this in the homeless person crying out old wounds. I see this in the eyes of the Chief Executive Officer going through a horrid divorce.

Am I lost?

Stability-healing heroes are here to heal. If I own a day with despair a hero helps inspires me to own a better tomorrow.

If my mood closes with despair I learn to open it with 333 healing.

I learn about transcending angel numbers.

On my transcending light quest I wrote my secrets into what I call a stability-healing diary.   I was on the trails in southern Virginia in pouring rain. Everything I owned was wet. I had come close to slipping off a cliff. I met a random couple at a trailhead. They were helping hikers. They gave out water and food. I accepted their offer to drive me to the hotel they were at and they offered to pay for my room. Their acts revealed my humanity compassion.

At night I played cards in the hotel lobby with this lovely couple from Colorado. I fondly remember how they owned their human compassion to a wet suffering stranger. This is one of many testimonials of humanities compassion.

Life's magical moments are not hidden in my day-to-day experiences. I open my eyes to see the light of joy in others and witness charities giving to strangers. These life experiences stick with me forever. I give joy and joy is given back. I create writings of inspiration and love.

TIP Δ – I learn how to open the deep spaces within to let more light and love in. My inner-self team can hold a lot of love.

TIP Δ – It heals me to create simple writings on paper and ink that reach a whole lot of people. I put my heart and soul into it!

I share my stability-healing diary with stability-healing heroes and my next day will get better. I never-give-up! The following defines my inner-self team who wrote my diary *Looking Glass Shattered*. This team remains inner-self true on my unique transcending journey.

Written by: Inner-Self Love
Written by: Inner-Self Playful
Written by: Voice Now Heard
Written by: Inner-Self Woman
Written by: Inner-Self Man
Written by: Inner-Self Forgiven
Written by: Others-Self Forgiven
Written by: My Human Compassion
Written by: Inner-Self Protected
Written by: Voice Now Validated
Written by: Compassion-Based Parent
Written by: Inner-Self Transcending

In the following picture I put the words "stay true" on my legs. I am staying true to my inner-self team! I took this picture while staying at the YMCA in Phoenix, Arizona. I am wearing the hiking boots I used on various hikes through Utah, Colorado, and Arizona.

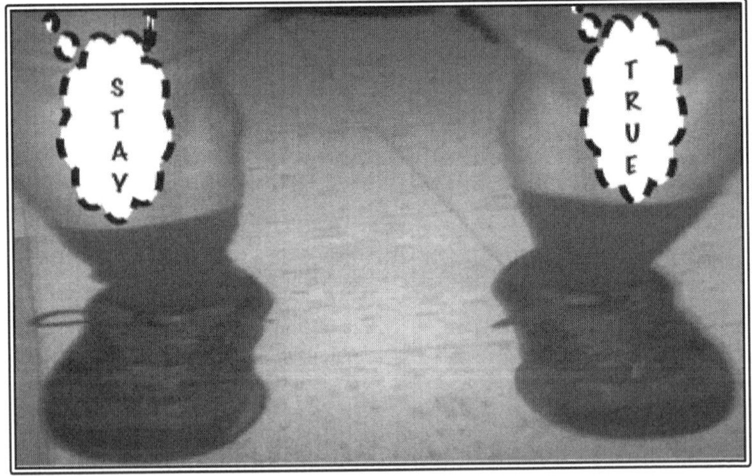

How can one transcending light quest heal Pangaea?

My diary words, art, and pictures own honest inner-self team moods. These are similar to what the following art illustrates.

The art shown above is by Steven Thompson mcdurphurp@gmail.com. His username is TranceParadox and website http://stproductions.snappages.com

I view the number 3 as it relates to my unique sense of communication, freedom, liberty, equality, justice, charity, and adventure. I own new life routines in response to the questions and answers discovered on my transcending light quest.

Congratulations! On December 12, 2012 Pangaea and humanities consciousness shifted. New events and experiences are happening. We live in evolutionary times. The possibilities of what each of us will do are beyond current understandings. We awaken to learn how to own a Transcended Champion well-being.

The orb has been associated with invisible spirits, auras, angels, healing, and energy. These are some orbs pictures I took on my transcending light quest. These two orbs were in front of a Midtown Atlanta, Georgia hotel.

This is blue and green energy orb I took a picture of in the courtyard at the Phoenix Arizona Art Museum.

Stability-Healing Questions

What is the MHC definition of hyper-paradise love?

How are external influences preventing MHC from healing?

How does inner-influenced actions help heal MHC?

How is MHC trying and failing better than doing nothing?

What are the core values of MHC?

How does set self-discipline help heal MHC?

How does well-being availability help heal MHC?

How does compassion-based listening help heal MHC?

Why does MHC own unconditional love disciplined?

What is the MHC definition of stability-healing heroes?

How can 119-fearlesness help heal MHC?

Who are the members of the MHC inner-self team?

How can honest diary entries help heal MHC?

Who are the names MHC writes into stone?

What does MHC see in the eyes of everyone?

Chapter 3 Stability-Healing Diary

I Am Blessed!
All My Senses
Loving Sight Smell
Sight Taste Touch
Transcending Light Vibrations
Healing Humanity Now
Hiking Nature Breathing!
Neutrally Clear Enlightened
Compassion-Based Listening
Well-Being Transcending
Child-Adult-Parent
Inner-Self Team
Voice Now Heard
All One Tribe
Shared Transcending Journeys
Ill To Healing
Whatever Crisis Arrives
Stability-Healing Heroes
Humanity Oneness Owned
Inner-Self Love

I did several class four River rafting trips in the southern United States. I rafted with five others and we had an experienced guide. Class four rapids own large volumes of wavy water, big drops, and rock hazards requiring careful maneuvering. It is dangerous and there are risks of serious injury or death. These rapids require everyone to wear a life vest.

My past white water rafting includes the class four Chattooga River in South Carolina. I finished the Arkansas River in Colorado. I completed the Ocoee River in Tennessee. I rafted a class four River near Calgary Canada.

I hiked the Appalachian Trail with three new friends. I suggested rafting the class four Nantahala River in North Carolina and I offered to pay their way. It was early in the season and the rafting company would only take me if I had three companions.

I paid for all of four of us to raft. It turns out none of my friends had rafted before. What a treat! We share wonderful bonding memories we will never forget and I finished another class four.

There was one section where the guide did some tricks so everyone fell out. When falling out we must go into a ball and never stand up! Many portions of the raging River have hidden underwater whirlpools that suck people in. They are so powerful it can pull someone underwater even if they are wearing a life vest. It only takes three minutes under water to die from drowning.

We are taught to never stand up because this increases the likelihood of getting a foot trapped under a rock. Heavy volumes of flowing water can easily cause a person to drown.

The safest maneuver when falling out is to be on the back and float down within the flow of the raging river. Make it to the safety of the shore as quick as possible!

I fell out of our raft during a class four rapid. The swirling waters flow disoriented me. I don't know if I am up or down. In those brief moments it's the same as jumping from a cliff or an airplane. Transcending light vibrations and angelic mists surround me. Time halts and I live in the now. I was outside the raft for a few moments yet it felt like years. Under water I am one with everything. I own an incredible lightness of being.

When I meditate in a fountain of oneness I transcend these same experiences. These are nurturing compassion-based moments with all of life's energy. Why do I participate in risky events?

It goes back to me saying, "Hi Mom!" before jumping from the airplane. She was extremely over protective of me due to an older brothers death. She owned fear from the abuse she faced in her childhood boarding school days. My Mom's overprotection and micromanagement of me pushed me into living a risky life.

Negative risk-taking and unstable well-being are at the roots of illness. In moments of exaggerated actions, I owned happy, sad, and anger all flooding into me at the same time. I have not always owned awareness of the state of my current well-being.

TIP Δ - I struggled with owning full awareness of my inner-self team. My honest questions and their answers own my unique healing.

Joy, anger, sad, love, happiness, fear plus the wheel of taste, touch, hearing, sight, and smell spin as one.

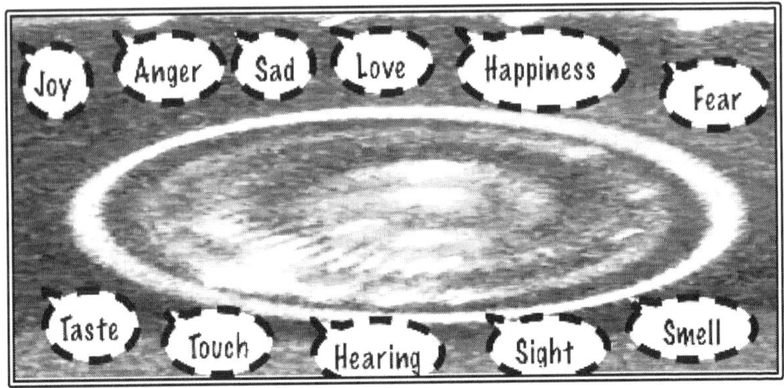

I owned change for different things at different times. This enrolls me into humanity. There are clear distinctions between what my well-being informs me and the actions I own based upon them.

How is my well-being?

Transcending light vibrations heal each of us. This light is all around us, in us, and among us. It is in city streets, amongst the vast wildernesses, and in every far corner of Pangaea. I can see our healing light. I just needed to learn how to look for it. This picture has transcending light vibrations in downtown Phoenix, Arizona.

TIP Δ - Great writing and speaking is not only what I write down or speak. This is also what I do not write and what I do not say.

I hold daily inner-self team project management meetings. I ask my inner-self team for their status updates. I am proud of myself for owning an active role in my healing.

Should I own action or own delay?

During my quest I fell in love with Hyper-Love Forgiven. We met in the summer of 2011 in Boston. I had asked her for directions to a local hostel. She immediately had me in her car, my backpack in the trunk, and she drove me to its location.

She had just left her Alcohol Anonymous (A.A.) meeting. A.A. holds meetings with men and women sharing their experiences with each other so they help support and solve their addictions.

I knew there was a reason why we met. I knew her in a past life. She reminded me of my oldest brother who suffers from alcohol addiction and has been drug free for the same amount of time she has. Healing is a theme of this diary so I believed being around her would give me ideas on how to finish my diary. Little did I know?

I floated on a cloud with Hyper-Love Forgiven. I mentioned I was interested in visiting New York City. She invited me to stay at her place. The immediate compassion and trust she gave me (a stranger in those brief moments) filled my loneliness with love.

I spent thousands staying at expensive hotels and condos while following her around New York and Vermont. I attempted to impress her. I bought a painting of hers for five thousand dollars. I gave her thousands for book illustrations I never received. I gave her clothing, jewelry, and paid off her police tickets. When our relationship fell apart I willingly gave her back everything she gave me. This relationship had no conditions and zero set-self discipline.

She told me the painting was thrown into a landfill by one of her friends. She said the illustrations were lost in the mail. She repeatedly told me she had six dollars in her account. She always needed money to pay for tickets or face jail.

I gave her thousands to prevent her from being homeless or imprisoned. The irony is I almost ended up homeless and bankrupt. I floated on hyper-paradise love. She was so exciting! The love I had for her was the same high as any drug. Some take illegal drugs to get high. Unconditional love without set self-discipline gave me this same high. I loved her much more than I loved myself.

I reveal my well being diary entries to trusted stability-healing heroes. My stability-healing diaries are my private property!

My diary writings own honesty and inner-self home openness.

Stability-healing diaries are for me to write down my journey. When the relationship I had with Hyper-Love Forgiven fell apart I found myself in crisis. I lacked stability-healing hero support.

There are past events I cannot talk about since they own abuse. These are societally embarrassing brain, senses, physical, and mobility challenges I do not want to reveal. No matter how wounding this healing process may be, I own my inner-self love and transcending light vibrations to help me heal old wounds.

TIP Δ – I reach out to stability-healing heroes for support.
TIP Δ – Old wounds enroll me in humanity and make me who I am.

I do not deny deeply buried wounds. I never suffer alone. My inner-self team grieves beyond old wounds. I prepare my daily healing work into a weekly schedule. I own multiple healing deadlines and change my healing priorities. These are examples of questions I must ask myself every day.

How is my well-being in the morning, daytime, and night?
Am I happy, sad, fearful, or in pain?
Why is my well-being changing?
My diary entries are my unique storytelling.

STORYTELLING

I write down my daily routines and relationship experiences. I determine if routines and relationships are either helping or hurting. I write my honest well-being updates. I am fair, forgiving, and loving to myself. I write what really happened throughout my day.

For example one day I came across three activists in front of the capital building in downtown Denver, Colorado. Our meeting reminds me of the urgency of helping our nation's homeless.

TIP Δ – Healing owns painful life truths so I must transcend them.
TIP Δ – I learn new healing tools to get to where I must be.

I will write more details of this quest in a screenplay. This will reveal more about the amazing events I encountered.

TIP Δ - I use colored ink pens to describe my current well-being.
I write angry moods with red ink.
I write happy moods using blue ink.
I describe sad moods with yellow ink.
I write unmet past and present needs using gold ink.
I write lessons learned using green ink.
I describe my healthy changes using silver ink.

TIP Δ - These are daily topic issues and the ink I write them in.

I nag my partner to clean and I am ignored. (Red ink)
My partner cleans without nagging and I am happy. (Blue ink)

TIP Δ - Points of present.

Why am I sad when my needs are not met? (Yellow ink)
I do compassionate compromise to own my needs. (Silver ink)

TIP Δ - Points of past.

I am angry with my partner for ignoring my needs. (Gold ink)

TIP Δ – Healthy lessons learned.

How do I stop my past from affecting my present? (Green ink)
How does anger affect my ability to own needs now? (Green ink)

TIP Δ - My daily healing summary.

I forgive all of my past unmet needs. (Silver ink)
The anger I had at my partner is due to my unmet needs. (Silver ink)

My life journey, actions, and results owned wounds. My story is the bitter and sweet life everyone knows. The suffering ownerships of my past lives, current life, and present living get erased into transcending light vibrations with no judgment. I was born to make mistakes and work through flaws. This is how my unique transcending journey gains compassion. Unique healing ideas appear as I am writing into my diary. If I own a certain well-being without knowing why I look deep inside to uncover the truth.

I focus on the areas I can improve upon. I write down whatever my current well-being status is without concern for legibility. At a later point in time, I go back and make my writings clearer.

My writings give me inner-self awareness. I write to own a better understanding of what "truthfully" happened. I never exaggerate away the truth of my old wounds. I must own honesty with what I write. Some of my past did get exaggerated to be worse than it was. Past pain overwhelmed me as yard trimmings can overflow a trashcan. This photo was taken outside a home in Atlanta, Georgia.

I remember learning new things. When I was a baby and food fell off my high chair I cried. As I aged into my toddler years I went about eating as if I had always known how. Embracing new ways to heal is the same thing. Once I own healing it's as if I always knew how. The comfort of healing is my top priority!

I own multiple diary copies. I use diary copies in healing ceremonies. New healing questions and answers surface. I add those truths into my healing education. My well-being transcending heals me throughout the day and night. I do inner-influenced actions so I am not a slave to how external influences need me to be. I focus on owning my needs instead of what others need from me. I am alive-owning-now with what is in my "now" moment.

While in the moment of crisis it is human nature to halt. I turn to stability-healing heroes to help reenergize my inner-self light bulb glow. This is the side of a bus I took in Denver, Colorado announcing an upcoming Christmas festival – Let It Glow 3 times!

TIP Δ - Stability-healing diaries reveal my life truths.

I take the time to complete my daily diary exercises. I take deep breaths and relax when necessary. My healing work can wear me down however love and compassion enables me to overcome.

I can heal my life.

TIP Δ - Those owning illness often lack required organizations to bringing in greater societal awareness for helping them own their needs and own a voice now validated.

I own a voice now validated to those with no voice. I climb mountains around Pangaea in tribute to Veterans, humanity, sensory stability heroes, healing, and compassion. Veterans give me my freedom and give me my needs. This is my picture at the peak of Mt. Bierstadt Colorado. My elevation is 14,060 feet. When I breathe at this altitude I am breathing oxygen at only around forty percent of the oxygen below 12,000 feet. The 12,000-foot elevation is tree line. Trees and most vegetation cannot survive above 12,000 feet. It is recommended to not live above tree line for too long.

I imagine I am an adult living in my former childhood home. I am reading through my diary. It describes all of my childhood to adult events. I flip through the pages to completely understand every word. My diary allows me to proudly display my journey. My life story goes into transcending light vibrations with no judgment.

I flip through the pages of my diary. Every page holding old wounds becomes blank. The compassions of transcending light vibrations healed and erased those pages.

External influences attempted to pull me away from writing my diary and doing the honest courageous work to heal. I go to stability healing heroes for support. My diary reveals the unique life I own. Each type of human healing and suffering is not the same.

While writing my diary pain came and went. My human compassion is here to help. I stop owning old wounded routines. My inner-self team light heals me in 201 and beyond. I am wearing happy New Year glasses in the New York City subway.

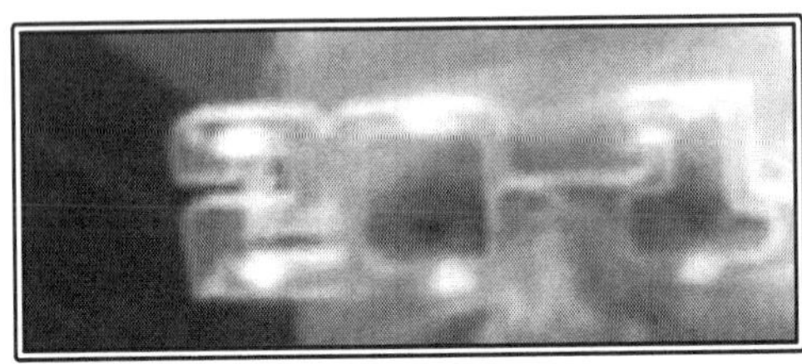

I wrote this diary entry before hiking the Appalachian Trail. I leave on April 1, 2011 from Hot Springs, North Carolina. What will I learn? I leave my life in Atlanta, Georgia behind. My unique transcending journey continues into the vast unknown. I quit a job that lacked challenges. I leave my despair in Atlanta, Georgia.

I owned a tight rope between a life I hate and finding my life purpose. I cut my current routines. I own a fear of what the trails might bring. I have an even greater fear in keeping myself in current habits. My honest courageous work is the freedom to know what to say and what to do. What conditions must I own to heal?

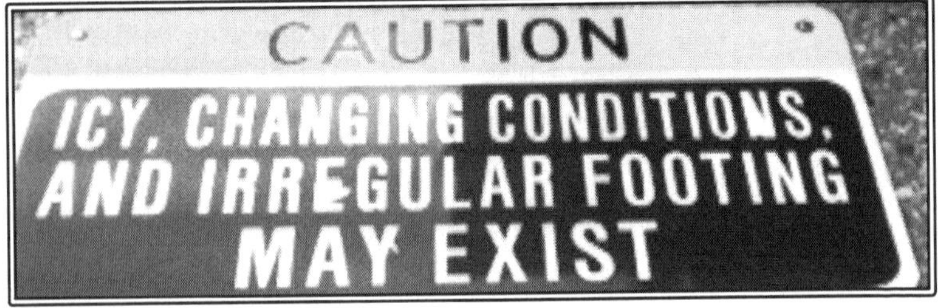

The answers to my conditions for me to heal are written into my diary. Owning love helps me heal. Illness and healing admit me into the tribe of humanity. I am proud to own flaws and own responsibility for my mistakes.

I love my individuality. There is no one else like me. I respect my need to be a unique individual who owns my life the way I need it to be. Each of us is born at a unique place and time. We transcend in a time nobody else has. I own never-give-up tools to bring high vibrational energy into my life. I took this photo of a streetlight located at Central Park, New York City.

TIP Δ – I am in awe of transcending light vibrational creations.
TIP Δ – Everyone belongs in transcending light vibrations.

I walk along a beach or mountain soaking in healing energy. I meditate to wondrous womb-healed soothing ocean waves. I love constant continual life change. I own awareness of my life purpose. My diary helps me observe and stabilize my well-being.

I know what it is like to love someone so much and to worry about him or her every step in my journey. Who? Hyper-Love Forgiven. I loved her so much and it made me sick to see how much of her life she had damaged. I could identify with this.

When she was a teenager her father threw her against a wall. She ran away from home with a boyfriend and had to run away from him after he abused her. Old wounds lead her to own addiction and lies.

Old wounds are viscous punishing circles of negative ancestry passed down from one generation to the next. I cannot tell where it begins or ends. Who started it? Who caused it? It is just there.

I needed to be the courageous male figure in her life protecting and healing her. I wanted to be the one person to give her everything - unconditionally.

It doesn't matter about my old wounds. What counts is they caused me decades of sufferings. I brought this upon myself.

Holding onto my old wounds brought people into my life who vibrated low energies of anger, blame, and guilt. I did not mean to hurt myself yet holding on to my old wounds were the survival method I knew best. I thought of old wounds as survival - eating and breathing. Without holding onto the vicious cycle of old wounds, the hurt of all my past years would overwhelm me.

My never-give-up approaches heal all this away.

I continue to randomly roam the country to complete this diary and heal myself. I learned from my parents divorce how easily any family member can do a permanent cord cut with another. Growing up in my family I was raised with despair, anger, and conflict. Family conflict and anger is a cancer leading to the break down of trust.

One day I do want to have children. This diary is my way of making Pangaea a better place so my children can live with more people owning inner-self love, compassion, and healing.

I hike with all my possessions in this transcending light quest backpack. I am searching for compassion and love. I always make a point to stop, breathe, and smell the flowers. This picture of MHC hiking the Appalachian Trails is my transcending light quest symbol.

I raise myself up to climb the tallest mountains. I rise up to survive the worst storms. I transcend to hike the hardest trails and live in any areas of a city.

When troubles may come I hike through crisis so I may find the safest and healthiest camping area. I followed this sign on the Appalachian Trails to find my camping spot.

Whether I am in the cities or at the wilderness our transcending 3, 333, and AUM are never far away. Here is another building in Phoenix, Arizona with a 333 address. I met a great healer at this location. When I began my journey I had no idea why I was so concerned about taking pictures of 333. The numbers 333 are the symbol of a woman or man who are Transcended Champions. My future diaries will teach me more about how to transcend into 333. This 333 status is when I become fully present and living in the now. It is living and leading my human compass and humanity in positive core values, set self-discipline, equal human civil rights, and stability.

Ancestors survive war, famine, and storms to give us birth. Ages of ancestral birth transcend each of us to be alive.

Ancestral stories of survival are miracles. Our collective ancestors creation of human civil rights is our greatest gift. This picture of blooming flowers is the MHC symbol of healing.

I honor our Veterans by hiking to the top of Piestewa Peak in Phoenix Arizona. It is named in honor of Army Spc. Lori Ann Piestewa, the first Native American woman to die in combat in the US military, and the first female soldier to be killed in action in the 2003 Iraq War.

Stability-Healing Questions

How can a stability-healing diary help heal MHC?

How does writing the well-being of MHC heal?

What are the ways MHC can live in the now?

How can diary entries help maintain the stability of MHC?

Who can MHC trust to reveal secret diary entries to?

What are the painful life truths MHC must confront?

How can MHC fit a healing schedule into daily routines?

What daily diary questions does MHC ask?

How does writing with different colored ink help heal MHC?

How does the uniqueness of MHC heal?

How can MHC stop old wounding actions and routines?

How can pride in MHC flaws heal?

How does MHC own stability?

What life challenges does MHC enjoy overcoming?

What is MHC in awe of?

Chapter 4 Human Civil Rights

How To Capture?
Heaven On Earth!
All Opens Up
Transcending Light Vibrations
Exemplified Through Nature
Glorified With Humanity
Illustrated In Space
Continuously Expanding Universe
Raw Pure Beauty
Within Every Soul
Rejoice and Remember
Alive-Owning-Now!
Inner-Self Love!

In every large city or small town on my unique 2,100-mile trek from Georgia to Maine and 2,778-mile trek from New York City to Los Angeles I made a point of visiting museums, monuments, parks, concerts, schools, people, and events I felt gravitated to.

I learned about Bahá'í while in Boston, Massachusetts. The Bahá'í accept the divinity of all major religious founders including Adam, Noah, Zarathustra, Krishna, Abraham, Moses, Buddha, Jesus, and Muhammad. Every prophet brings humanity a new transcending for the time and place they were on earth. They believe that there will be new prophets to add to this list. It is a distinct religion with scriptures, teachings, laws, and history. I share their beliefs that all the essential love and compassion religious teachings heal us.

Attending these types of events brought me a "University of Generous Knowledge". I learned much more from my transcending light quest then my four-year education at the University of Tennessee! I showed up to many new places with a clear open "baby sponge like mind". I breathed in everything I needed to learn.

I was in Washington D.C. on Memorial Day 2011. I stumbled into an amazing event. I happened to be at the Washington D.C. National Mall and there were motorcycle-riding Veteran Stability Heroes from all over the nation. Fifty thousand riders! This sight sent a huge chill up my spine. I gave Veterans a high five as they drove by.

I want Veterans to get all the praise and thank you they deserve. They gave up all their freedoms so civilians may own ours. Tears came to my eyes as I watched in pride of all Veterans who were there to represent every extremist war over the last seventy years.

I struck up conversation with a man next to me. We were discussing the ideas of money and homelessness. I told him how shocked I was too view so many homeless Veterans in Washington D.C. I see this sight and I own shame about my country.

He said to me, "You don't need to fear money and homelessness. Money will come to you. You need to take this time to really enjoy your sabbatical and lead a new life purpose. You need to live your life as you see fit and then money will come. If you live in constant fear of going broke and homeless you will never live the life you were meant to have."

I also visited the museum of robotics on the campus of the Massachusetts Institute of Technology (MIT) in Boston, Massachusetts. Wow! I am shocked to see all the latest and greatest technology invented and the new things coming out soon! I did the Harvard tour and I felt surprised to hear of so many successful people to have either graduated from there or dropped out to go on to success.

I had just visited everything I needed to see in Boston. I had just set my new goal of transcending to the top of Mount Katahdin in Maine. I decided I was going to make it no matter what! With no planning "whatsoever" I take buses up to Portland Maine.

Once at Portland I took buses all the way to the Baxter State Park area. I get off the bus and meet a guy named Stan. I strike up conversation about transcending the mountain and he is there for the same thing. After a short while, a man named Jerry picks us up. He runs the Hostel based at the bottom of the mountain. I had dinner with Dan that night and we were at the same Hostel. I had so many of these helpful moments on my quest I no longer call it coincidence, synchronicity, fate, or fortune. I must call this the help from our shared divine angels.

I had a room in the Hostel even though it was peak season. I found the irony in that we are both named Dan and have several things in common. Dan and I are at the same age and seeking something more from life. We were both in the Boy Scouts and we were back at the trails for giving our mid-life direction some answers. I would love to see Dan again one day.

We had a great stay at the hostel. I am most thankful for the huge breakfast I had the morning before our transcending. Dan and I went together first thing in the morning. This is about a thirteen mile round trip hike. Many hikers do not make it in one day.

As we transcend, Dan and I discuss love, life, work, and the Boy Scouts. We push and pull our bodies over every granite stone. At the beginning of our ascent we hike over medium sized stones. As we near the summit each of those stones get much larger. Now we are transcending up boulders. We must do hand over handwork to get up and over. Many boulders have embedded metal posts so we grab those and hoist ourselves up.

As we are close to the summit I look down and see a most glorious sight! Clouds, hundreds of them are below my field of vision. I see sky above the clouds. I keep telling myself I got to reach the very top. I got to make it to the end of this Appalachian Trail of which I hiked it's beginning so many times before. At the top of Katahdin there is a placard officially stating that this is the end of the Appalachian Trail. Many through hikers having done the three to six month hike from Georgia to Maine have cried at this sign. Their mood at the finish line can be overwhelming!

The two Dan's made it to the very top! It is momentarily the gorgeous clear weather we enjoyed at its base. By the time we turn to leave the summit fast moving clouds surround us. I am one with mist of transcending light vibrations again. The same as when I was in North Carolina. It was careful hiking to make it through thick clouds. I could only see my hand in front of my face. I was "careful" to step through one boulder at a time. One wrong step and my head might fall into a rock below.

These hikes in the woods enabled my senses to become more aware, more intense, and clear. I am not thinking of the past or future. All I can focus on is my now. I have to survive! My wits are helping me make the right steps.

I talked with Dan about camping overnight at the base however after reaching the top I knew what I had to do. I had to work on my company and finish this diary. I got what I needed from the Appalachian Trails for now. I needed new challenges.

I walked from the base of the mountain to the nearest road. A young couple where heading to the coast of Maine to a beautiful town named Belfast. They offered me a ride and off I went.

The girlfriend of the driver saw me worn out and tired and owned her my human compassion to give me (stranger) a ride. I was thankful I was being helped and did my best to ignore our speed.

We were traveling in an old rusted out car at over a hundred miles an hour. This five-hour drive took about three hours. I had bought a brand new pair of hiking boots before transcending Mount Katahdin. They were completely worn out by the time I did the round trip. They say no one is ever the same after hiking Katahdin.

I loved Belfast Maine. I spent several days there and I went with some new friends to another gorgeous Maine spot. We went to the top of Bar Harbor Maine. What gorgeous sites Maine has!

TIP Δ – I went with transcending light vibrations faith and no fear.

Shambhala is a Sanskrit term of any home owning peace, tranquility, and happiness. The rains of shambhala had washed away my suffering. When I open myself up to our continuously expanding universe I was God helped me in owning my goals.

Each of us is a proud member of humanity. Human civil rights are given to us in the womb. My transcending light quest had me own greater appreciation of our shared human civil rights.

My umbilical cord is cut and I go into the hands of strangers. My healed womb vanishes as I confront life. It is an amazing journey each of us treads. The blank page of birth gives me a start. Where do I go from birth? Do I tread lightly? Do I walk with a force forever healing Pangaea?

Human civil rights leaders forever changed Pangaea. Their honest courageous work opened the doors to allow each and every one of us an ability to own our needs. Humanity can work harder at owning wider human civil rights for all. This is my agenda in the year 201 ॐ and beyond.

Human civil rights are equality for all women and men regardless of sexual orientation, race, age, disability, national origin, religion, ethnicity, and caste. Every human has the right to the freedoms of speech, voting, religion, press, right to self-defense, right to privacy, right to fair trail, and assembly.

TIP Δ – Before human civil rights were enacted into law humanity lived as cave women and cave men. We must own forever-clear liberty, equality, justice, and freedom - forever!

The only thing I fear is losing human civil rights. The unique transcending journey of humanity must reverse 911 thinking to own first nation-healing 119-fearlessness. Let us come together to regain inner-self child-like innocence to trust humanity.

I learned to love my inner-self team. I freed my life from negative ancestral messages. Now my friends and family see me for the compassionate person I am. I avoid inner-self team judgments, and anger. My inner-self team unites me to be beautifully human!

The transcending equality template defines the stars, sun, and the beautiful earth itself. It owns the set-self discipline of my actions and results. This template history includes countless millions of shared humanity ancestors born into the continent of Africa. Africa is where I believe all humanity evolved.

TIP Δ - These are transcending equality template ownerships.

Owning constant nature changes and weather changes.
Owning continuously transcending light vibrations changes.
Owning gender, race, and culture.
Owning womb-birth, actions, results, and death.

The late 1960s were the start of my womb birth. Swimming around in the womb was a start to life. I floated in warm, compassion-filled juices owning my needs. Here is a time when my well-being owned healed. My womb-healed days are not long ago. I recall womb-healed ownership into my adult years.

Human civil rights movements carved a unique tattoo into my journey. I was born in the 1960s after many important leaders died. Their passions for human civil rights were born into me. Every baby born in a certain era absorbs the occurrences going on at that time.

Each of us is frustrated!

Transcending light vibrations exists within every umbilical cord attachment to humanity. I am of the first generation born at the start of human civil rights. Every human is equal despite flaws, nationality, backgrounds, race, gender, caste, ancestry, sexual orientation, or where we live. These are womb birth guaranteed human civil rights each of us own; needs, medications, stability, liberty, equality, justice, freedom, and meaningful work we love.

Everyone asks these anxiety-filled questions.

How can my family and I own stability?
How can I own my needs and the needs of my descendants?

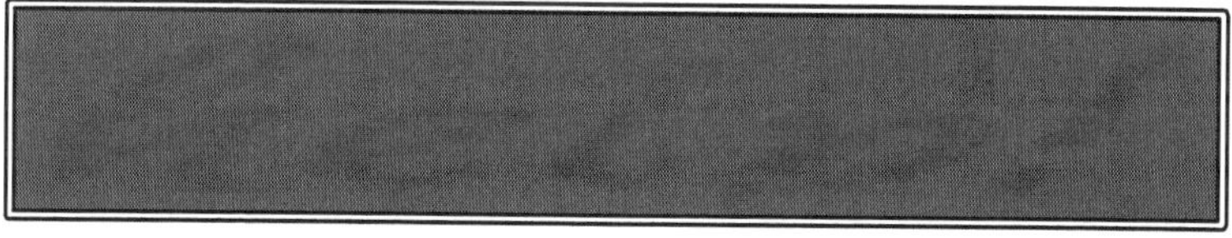

Sensory stability heroes are labeled handicapped, disabled, mentally ill, or in recovery. They might endure challenge in owning needs. If a person does not own needs the long-term results can be institutionalization, homelessness, and early death. I view our heroes as clearly as I see myself. We can implement new proactive programs and heal our heroes. Too many Veterans become sensory stability heroes. Heroes can lack crucial support from government, family, and friends.

Everyone has been a baby unable to survive without help. Each of us spends a lifetime between owning healed and owning ill. Each of us has been every gender, caste, race, nationality, transgender, and sexual orientation in a past life.

TIP Δ - Humanity owns equality when we own these life truths.

Pangaea has gone between owning national and individual freedoms. When Pangaea is threatened with its safety, many nations put laws into place limiting individual freedoms including freedoms of assembly and freedoms of speech. They are allowed this under the facade of fighting terrorists. We must learn to fight the terrorists with everything we have but also grant our citizens the freedoms the humanity has worked so hard at to get to where we are right now. I will volunteer to be in the armed forces. I want to go over and fight the terrorists with everything I have.

Individual freedom is everyone's equal freedom to speak and assemble with a voice now heard. It "is not" the freedom to be lazy and uninvolved. It "is not" having our own needs over others. It "is not" not freedom to force our ways at the expense of others.

Where do you think our Pangaea human civil rights are now?

TIP Δ – Owning these personal transformations changes adversity.

Slavery To Freedom
Poverty To Wealth
Illness To Health
Anger To Compassion
War To Peace

I become more involved. I am able to help humanities transcending journey to own equal human civil rights for all. Human civil rights are vital for all transcending light journeys.

I believe Pangaea human civil rights have become tilted.

What humanity journey cautions must be owned?

I welcome your thoughts on improving human civil rights.

I am excited to wake up and learn more.   I check compassion into my inner-self team. I took this photo at a Phoenix, Arizona art museum locker.

While in Atlanta, Georgia, I had a conversation with a man in his sixties who is campaigning for same sex marriage. He described terrifying events of living in the south during the nineteen-fifties. In these days he had to meet secretly with friends who were working to own same sex marriage into law. He talked of beatings, discrimination, and secrecy.

I told him I am writing a book about healing and human civil rights. He mentioned there is a big difference between tolerance and acceptance. Our conversation had made me think carefully about the definition of these words.

I decided to add ownership into our discussion. Ownership is the next step to where our collective equal human civil rights must go. How are tolerance, acceptance, and ownership defined?

Tolerance is respecting all races, castes, and sexual orientation.
Tolerance is respecting all humans equally.
Acceptance is when laws pass to protect humanity.
Ownership is when I know where humanity must go.
Ownership is helping all others own their needs.
Ownership is helping pass humanity healing laws.
Ownership is helping all diversity of humanity to own healing.

I took a picture of my hand with the phrase "I love diversity!"

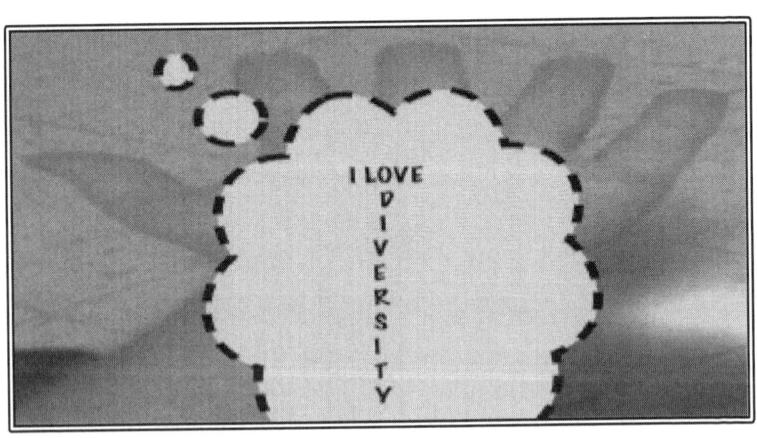

TIP Δ – We are one-Tribe, one-First Nation, and one-Pangaea!

When I take myself to the present moment I own the transcending light vibrations in everything and everyone. These vibrations give each of us free will of how to think and how to act. I learn to cut low vibrational wounding attachments to fear, anger, crisis, and constant inner-self mind chatter.

Had I known of the healing approaches in this diary I would have been better prepared. I am equipped on my unique transcending journey by owning my new healing tools. My life is transcending approach brings personal life transformations.

The number three heals me and fits me perfectly. I took this picture at a Denver, Colorado thrift store where I had to buy new clothes. I arrived in Denver from Harpers Ferry West Virginia with a few items of clothing.

Old wounding definitions of how I viewed life brought me unnecessary suffering. I heal when I learn what "life is".

TIP Δ – Humanity rises up to meet the standards of our leaders. If leaders think their citizens do not care or are not compassionate then our leaders will not care or own compassion. I need humanity to have compassion-based leaders who do care.

Many thoughts occur as I go through my day. I can go from sad to happy and then happy to sad. My well-being changes as I own my needs, lose my needs, talk with a negative person, or associate with positive folks. These cause my inner-self team third-eye light bulb AUM energy to vibrate at dim, on, or off. An uplifting movie can turn my inner-self light bulb on. I read a tragic news story and my inner-self light bulb energy goes to dim or maybe even off. Extreme flips of my inner-self light bulb energy causes instability.

I am surrounded with entertainment where main characters end the movie by walking off to a happy future while destroying negative monsters. Fantasy based super heroes fighting monsters influence me to own a looking glass fantasy. If I view life as exaggerated sad, happy, fearful, courageous, and or negative I own despair.

Life Is Transcending!

Life is transcending tools give me an ability to walk past chaos to find and open my looking glass shattered door of reality. I open my transcended door, walk in, and own a super star life.

The art shown above is by Steven Thompson mcdurphurp@gmail.com. His username is TranceParadox and website http://stproductions.snappages.com.

Stability-Healing Questions

How are transcending light vibrations healing MHC?

How does MHC define equal human civil rights?

What are the ideals of Shambhala healing MHC?

How does equal human civil rights help heal MHC?

Why are treading with big footprints important to MHC?

How did 911 affect human civil rights?

How did equal human civil rights arrive into MHC?

What is 119-fearlessness and how does it heal MHC?

How is the transcending equality template healing MHC?

How can humanity defend and extend human civil rights?

What anxiety filled questions does MHC ask?

What proactive human civil rights solutions does MHC suggest?

How does MHC define sensory stability heroes?

How can tolerance, acceptance, and ownership heal humanity?

Chapter 5 Life Is Transcending

Danny Is Transcending
3rd Eye Journey
I Look Behind
Stability-Lessons Learned
Viewing The Sky
Night Owns Day
Day Owns Night
Forever Changing Clouds
Purple Swirled Gold
What Is Overcast?
Soon Becomes Clear
Pangaea Continual Transcending
Every New Day!
Another Erasing Begins
Neutral Clear Enlightened
Compassion-Based Transcending
Lovingly Redrawn Again
Look Now Behold
333 Compassion Awareness
Questions And Answers
Life Truths Owned!

This is one of many addresses my transcending light quest came across. This is the Hindu temple in Atlanta, Georgia where I went with friends. I got an important education here.

The womb is a beautiful place for a baby before beginning their unique transcending journey. The womb is even more beautiful when one emerges as an equal, accepted, and loved member of the first nation-tribe of humanity. This is my human inner-self transcending. The inner-self team 3 = AUM attaches my third-eye to humanity, inner-self love, and our shared transcending light vibrations. This is a picture of me wearing a skydiving harness. It is March 2011 and right before I jumped out of an airplane.

TIP Δ – Everyone owns questions, answers, talking, and listening on their journey. These four modalities enable transcending.

MHC is an adventurer spirit, poet, scholar, healer, and Indigo. My Human Compassion learns to evolve beyond fearing, beyond pop culture, beyond external influences, beyond attachments, and beyond nationality. I strive for transcending. I own the ideals, identity, and symbols of My Human Compassion. The symbol of MHC lives beyond the time when my human ashes are spread amongst Pangaea.

It is easy for me to forget I live within transcending light vibrations. Everything might seem stagnant yet I focus on seeing new life changes. I chose my parents to help me develop my natural abilities. I needed "extra" work on my unique transcending journey.

I am an Indigo with aura warrior leadership. I stand up and fight for what I believe is fair. I will not be lied to or manipulated. I do not agree with dysfunctional systems. I am here to reveal antiquated systems in schools, government, parenting, and healthcare.

TIP Δ – MHC will help Pangaea vibrate at higher energies!

I own a deep blue indigo aura of intensity, clairvoyance, and healing. I am learning about them. I will write more of what I learn in later diaries. I must learn to access new levels of consciousness. I raise every consciousness to a higher vibrational frequency.

I am passionate in my beliefs. I need to own the truth and break down old ways of thinking. I will create a path to help others see Pangaea at a higher level of transcending. I will teach more about love and abundance in our Age of Aquarius.

I never lose sight of who I am. I am drawn to owning strength and courage from being myself. I know that things will improve as I breathe in more of my "I am Presence". I am blessed to help humanity and lead others on a new mission. I own the strength and wisdom for this. I am fortunate to lead and never give up.

I need art, philosophy, stories, adventure, acting, singing, and music. I attach to our divine and everything as pure blue energy.

Pangaea energy is changing. I must tune into this and the new beliefs I was not raised with. I am not perfect and I try to do what is best. Humanity is going through evolutionary times and we are all evolving to be fully conscious beings.

When aliens land on earth *Looking Glass Shattered* is the writings they must own. This diary can save humanity. Aliens might have already landed; in fact each human might be an alien? I do not know the answer to this. I have not come across any aliens so far. I do hope to meet some. I will be certain to write about this!

In February of 2012 I had to move back to my hometown. Hyper-Love Forgiven and I had broken off our relationship. This sent me into despair. I believed we would become a family one-day. I needed tools to get beyond crisis. I struggled to own happiness.

Every town seemed to have a problem yet I had Hyper-Love Forgiven by my side. When I left her, I realized it was never the place owning flaws. I owned old wounds in need of healing. I was in love with someone without unconditional love disciplined. I attempted to make it into something it could never be.

I learned life is not fair or unfair. War, poverty, super storms, crime, the poisoning of our environment, children needlessly dying of starvation, wealthy refusing to donate to charity, and needless violence are in our reality. Poor own fewer chances to own their needs than rich. The fantasy of life being fair or unfair does not exist. If fair exists who decides fair or not fair?

I cannot base my life on ideas of others being fair or unfair. If friends, family, jobs, or dating relationships end, this has nothing to do with life being fair or unfair. These ended because I vas vibrating into my life other people who owned the lower energies of anger, resentment, shame, and blame. I intentionally entered wounded relationships because I needed to maintain my old wounds.

February 2012 marked a time when I owned challenges. I believed the next town owned a chance for me to own a home. This next town never came. A person owning anger is represented by the words wrong, bad, and ill. A person owning compassion is represented by right, good, and healthy. Heaven or Hell can be life on earth depending on a person owning compassion or anger.

My inner-self home owns 333 = 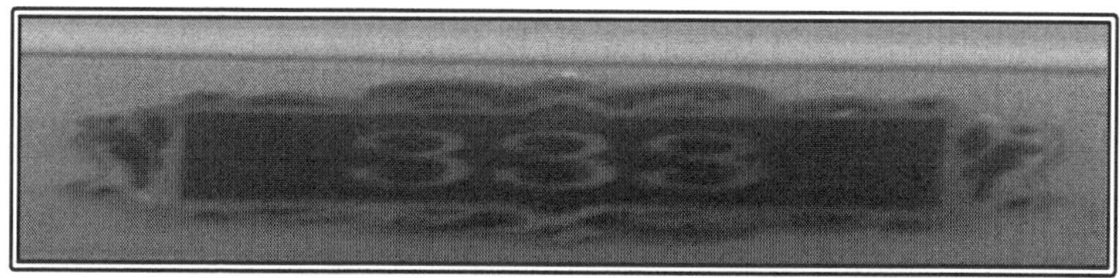 cords. This is a hotel room I visited in Denver, Colorado.

Life is transcending is based on everything my six senses own. These include a consciousness of my well-being (stable, unstable, or a range within stability), consciousness of my joints and muscles in action, consciousness of my sense of balance, consciousness of my body in space (lying down or jumping), sight, touch, taste, smell, and hearing. This includes the sense owned when I transcend my umbilical cord attachments by owning pure inner-self love and unconditional love from our transcending light vibrations.

Positive things happen to positive people. Positive things happen to negative people. Negative things happen to positive people. Negative things happen to negative people. Life is not fair or unfair. All of these represent the life is transcending approach.

The house I grew up in is no longer there and my parents I knew as a child are gone. Spring turns to summer and summer to fall.

My unique transcending journey owns positive changes.

Stability-healing heroes own positive core values and help guide me. I have attempted to hide honest well-being availability; however this wounds me more. I learn to allow my inner-self team to own a life is transcending approach. I proudly say yes or no to everything coming my way. My inner-self team has new management. I call my inner-self team using my 333-333-3333 of inner-self love. I took this picture at Aurora, Colorado.

I hike my journey following my life is transcending signs.
This is one beautiful hike at Moab Utah in Arches National Park.

TIP Δ - The following describes the communicator types.

An aggressive talker cannot own set self-discipline.
An aggressive talker dominates others and loses relationships.
An unprotected talker lets aggressive talkers dominate them.
Compassion-based communicator's own well-being available talking and compassion-based listening.

TIP Δ - Aggressive or unprotected communicators lose trust.

My positive relations share well-being availability and compassion-based compromise. Aggressive and unprotected communicators own life as puppets having inner-self team strings pulled by others. I took this photo at a festival in Atlanta Georgia.

I observe aggressive or unprotected communicators as being more likely to own instability. Is the person I am with an aggressive, unprotected, or compassion-based communicator?

TIP Δ – This is well-being available talking.

I defend myself and avoid aggressive communicators. I communicate my current well-being with those I trust. I own my needs based on compassion-based compromise. I set self-discipline with my inner-self team and others.

Well-being available talking cuts through all my inner-self team trivia and lets my compassion shine!

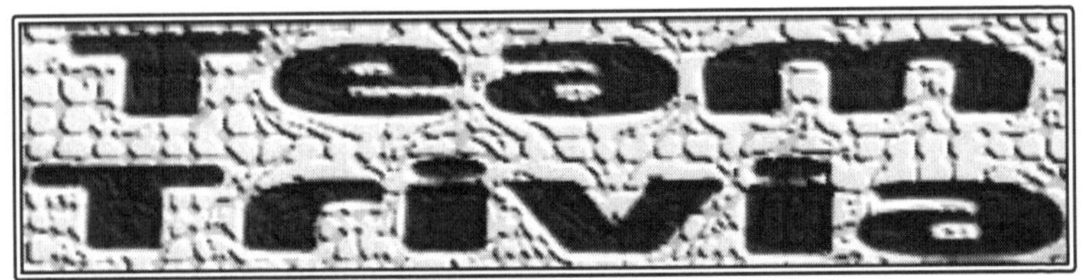

TIP Δ – This owns compassion-based communication.

Δ person I communicate with might say angry things at me. My inner-self team learns to respond with compassion. There is pain in the angry person I communicate with. I give others a chance to express their suffering. I own compassion-based listening. I never listen in order to judge, blame, or shame others. I listen to offer others a chance to express their needs. I give others a chance to express their voice now heard. I am listening to relieve pain and understand others. I often speak with a person owning pain.

TIP Δ – I always own my inner-self love and high vibrational energy no matter the energy level of the person I am with. I own compassion to help others heal old wounds. MHC is proud to support stability-healing hero friendships.

I am proud to support veteran stability heroes. They sacrifice their needs so civilians own ours. I will help start organizations to heal heroes fighting our extremist wars.

I learn to own awareness of myself and take care of my needs. This allows me to be more compassionate and own inner-self love. Other people benefit from my presence and I can help others.

I can never fully understand the life of another. Compassion-based listening is my tool to try and understand.

TIP Δ – Questions, answers, talking, and listening are the four major tools, which are helping me transcend on my journey!

TIP Δ – My inner-self love helps me own a better everyday life.

TIP Δ – I own responsibility for my troubles and mistakes.

A defining event occurring to me at age seven was when a neighborhood kid persuaded me to throw rocks over cars driving in the street. I knew this violated my core values. I did this to be a cool kid like my friend. A few minutes went by and danger came my way. I did not think through the results of my actions using my core values. I did not set self-discipline and say no to my friend's advice.

A driver saw the rocks flying over his car. He slammed on his brakes. My friend took off on his bike as fast as he could. I felt I had nowhere to go because I was in front of my family home. A tall stranger picked me up and held me in an iron grip. I alone faced the wrath of this crazed lunatic lunging from his Pinto. I was left to face abuse with no one to protect me. The other kid got away with it.

The stranger said, "Where do you live?" "Well, I said with a trembling voice," "This is my house." He picked me up and dragged me to the front door and rang the bell. My father came to the door and saw sheer rage upon this stranger's face. My father bowed submissively to this man and did not protect me. If my father does not protect me why should I protect myself?

It was an eye opener. After seeing the submissiveness of my father and hearing my frightened apology, the stranger returned to his car and drove off. I did not own an inner-self protected. I owned fear and anxiety. My inner-self home was up for sale.

Life is not fair!

The life is not fair theme vibrated within me during my darkest despair. I didn't understand why others could avoid punishment for the same actions I did. I used to believe comic book ideals stating life is fair and justice always triumphs. The super hero always destroys the monster at the end? How is life supposed to be?

Is life supposed to be sad or happy?
Is life supposed to be unfair or fair?
Is life supposed to be angry or compassionate?
Is life supposed to be fearful or courageous?
Is life supposed to be negative or positive?

My life is transcending approach is life can be sad or happy, angry or compassionate, fearful or courageous, negative or positive. It is up to everyone to own inner-self love so happy, thankful, and positive successes come into our lives.

I carry a strip of clothing saying the word "courage" through much of my quest. This is my constant reminder of courage through crisis. This saying reminds me of my honest courageous work to heal. I drink from my AUM healing cup.

COURAGE

TIP Δ – As an adult, I can walk away from dangerous situations.

As my inner-self team aged, I still felt as a wounded twelve-year-old in the body of an adult. This caused me unnecessary suffering. Anger made it hard for me to own healed turns on my journey. This is the New York City library where I worked on this diary.

Free from the womb. I enter transcending light vibrations. I own womb birth guaranteed human civil rights. My ancestors and their first nation-healing live within. Inner-self love guides me beyond the push/pull of old wounds.

The years before I took this quest I was looking glass lost. This quest is how I found my inner-self team. This picture is my transcending light quest tattoo. I am wandering but I am not lost. Spiritual energy is everywhere to help guide me.

Taking many forms of public transportation across this country helped me learn the life is transcending approach. I took this picture as I was getting off of a bus in Denver, Colorado. I questions, answered, talked, and listened to many people across the USA while taking public transportation.

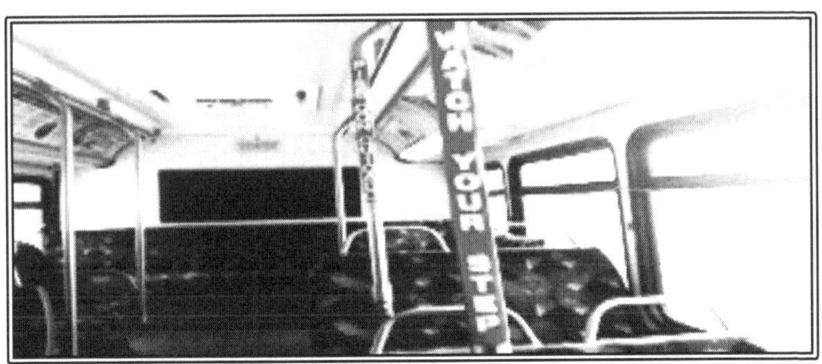

I own love for my ancestors. All faced unique struggles. Each one did the best they could to own their needs and help me with owning my needs. I offer first nation-healing names to detail their unique life. What is in a name? A whole lot of first-nation-healing!

Stability-Healing Questions

How does life is transcending approach heal MHC?

Why is it hard for MHC to let go of old wounds?

How can unconditional love disciplined heal MHC?

Why did MHC attract wounded people?

How does MHC heal with compassion?

What are the communicator types?

How does MHC define compassion-based listening?

What is well-being availability?

Who are the heroes MHC is proud to support?

How can "life is not fair" help heal MHC?

How does courage help heal MHC?

What made the inner-self home of MHC up for sale?

What external things made MHC energy glow dim and off?

Chapter 6 First Nation-Healing

Danny Loves Ancestors
Past Present Future
Stone Pond Together
Ancestral Tribal Inheritances
Humanity Lives Here
Death And Life
Generations Of Ancestors
Known And Unknown
Owning Womb-Healed!
Love Acceptance Shared
Humans Represent Stones
Ancestors Represent Pond
Stone Needs Pond
Pond Needs Stone
Positive Ancestral Inheritances
Strive For More!
Unique Transcending Journey
All Shared Compassions

I was raised as an atheist and all life answers must be solvable in scientific intellectual "provable" based solutions. There must be proof and everything must be tangible.

As I progressed on my transcending light quest I opened up my beliefs and realized the truths surrounding Pangaea. A new reality zapped into my awareness. I call this first nation-healing.

I am a creation of untold billions of ancestors over eons of time. I believe everyone shares these same ancestors. I cannot choose my living or dead ancestors

What sufferings, failures, or successes did my ancestors own?
How did they heal and overcome challenges?
Who did what to whom?

TIP Δ - I will never know answers to these questions.

TIP Δ - I own forgiveness to my ancestors.

TIP Δ - They did there best given their ancestral inheritance.

TIP Δ - I am thankful to my ancestors for giving me life.

I took this picture of an Egyptian Hieroglyph at the Museum of Art in New York City. These types of tablets in ancient times were used for diaries and storytelling. This is what first nation storytellers used across Pangaea. Tablets passed down ancestral teachings from one generation to the next. This informs a future generation about past mistakes and how to avoid them. This is an important way our civilizations could advance.

TIP Δ – Owning ancestral forgiveness sets me free.

TIP Δ – Owning ancestral forgiveness sets descendants free.

Everyone receives negative and positive ancestral inheritance messages. Everyone alive is a creation of ages of evolution. Birth is a miracle! Ancestors survived ages of plague, storms, war, and famine to give us life. I believe all of our ancestors originated from Africa. Everyone has slightly different features yet we are the same.

First nation-healing tribal customs dictate newborn babies receive names based on what traits their ancestors desire them to own. Names are lovingly transferred from one ancestor to the next.

First nation-healing teaches we are born with names our parent's choose for us. We are also born with transcending light vibrational names. These names guide us to owning our unique life purpose. We are challenged to own our transcending light names.

TIP Δ – These are my first nation-healing inner-self child names.

Inner-Self Love
Inner-Self Playful
Voice Now Heard

TIP Δ – These are my first nation-healing inner-self adult names.

Inner-Self Woman
Inner-Self Man
Inner-Self Forgiven
Others-Self Forgiven
My Human Compassion

TIP Δ – These are my first nation-healing inner-self parent names.

Inner-Self Protected
Voice Now Validated
Compassion-Based Parent
Inner-Self Transcending

I am jet skiing on a great day in lake Altoona Georgia.
My inner-self playful child is out to have fun and own play!

Everyone might believe they own first nation-attachments to Asia, Africa, Americas, Europe, or Australia. The life is transcending approach teaches we own first nation-attachments to the tribe of humanity. First nation-healing names are my transcending.

I deliver my ancestral inheritance into my diary.

TIP Δ – This is my Inner-Self Child and Inner-Self Playful.

I own child-like trust to attach with new cord relationships.
I explore everything around me with no fear.
I am emboldened with a fun, good-natured, and humorous life.

TIP Δ – This is my Inner-Self Child and Inner-Self Love.

I am transcending based on my inner-self approval.
I own stability to own my needs.
I own inner-self love for myself without any conditions.
I own the love of our transcending light vibrations.

TIP Δ – This is my Inner-Self Child and Voice Now Heard.

I let my inner-self child speak up and be heard without fear.
I let my inner-self child speak and trust that others listen.

TIP Δ – This is my Inner-Self Adult and Inner-Self Woman.

I love feminine and it's compassionate creation.

TIP Δ – This is my Inner-Self Adult and Inner-Self Man.

I love masculine and it's compassionate creation.

TIP Δ – This is my Inner-Self Adult and Inner-Self Forgiven.

I forgive the times my relationships ended in failure.
I let go of all of my past failures and mistakes.
I own my flaws and do my best to overcome them.
I make relationships work based on my inner-self approval.
I take a job solely based on my inner-self approval.

TIP Δ – This is my Inner-Self Adult and Others-Self Forgiven.

I forgive abuse, chaos, and crisis others gave me.
I forgive others for teaching me crisis and chaos is okay.
I forgive others for giving me anger instead of compassion.

TIP Δ – This is my Inner-Self Adult and My Human Compassion.

I do my best to understand the sufferings of others.
I own zero judgments, zero blame, and zero anger.
I own compassion for myself and compassion for humanity.

TIP Δ – This is my Inner-Self Parent and Inner-Self Protected.

I maintain my stability-healing diary.
I own set self-discipline to protect my stability.
I attach positive cords relations and cut negative cord relations.
I own stable-senses tools and positive actions.
My actions and results are grounded on my inner-self approval.

TIP Δ – This is my Inner-Self Parent and Voice Now Validated.

I own a voice now heard filled with safety, acceptance, and stability.
I speak using a voice constructed on 119-fearlessnesss.
I own a voice now validated to help others.

TIP Δ – This is my Inner-Self Parent and Compassion-Based Parent.

I teach positive core values and how to own inner-self love.
I educate others on first nation-healing, compassion, and healing.

TIP Δ – This is my Inner-Self Parent and Inner-Self Transcending.

I transcend my inner-self love as seeker and teacher.
I transcend my inner-self love to heal humanity and Pangaea.

All of my first-nation names live in my inner-self-home.
I enter my inner self-home.   I am here!

I found my first-nation names so I can own a stable inner-self home.

Compassion is how I parent my inner-self team and parent others. I am thankful to own awareness in every new day. As an adult, I reunite with my inner-self playful child by observing other children chasing kites and making sand castles.

My parents owned their lives as wounded twelve-year-olds in the body of adults. When I was fifteen, my parents divorced and this gave me wounds. I lived with Abusive Father Forgiven to avoid the rage of Angry Mother Forgiven. I had to make it clear to Abusive Father Forgiven he could dominate me. I could have passed on the wounds of my parents to my future children but I said no to that and created this diary instead. My teenage years lacked a safe place to park my inner-self home.

TIP Δ - Angry Mother Forgiven/Mother Loves Child.

In my teenage years my Mother put mismanaged rage on my. My Dad wouldn't own my Mom's anger so she gave it to me. She owned past abuse by my father, childhood, and ancestry. She owned a wounded child in the body of an adult.

Do you know an angry Mother forgiven?

How could they have replaced anger with owning compassion?

TIP Δ - Genius Missed Potential/Uncle Loves Nephew.

He had huge success and managed a university at one time.
His self-righteous know-it-all traits cost him jobs and relations.
He declared bankruptcy, was an alcoholic, and divorced.
He owned a wounded child in the body of an adult.

Do you know a genius with missed potential?
What tools could they have owned to be successful?

TIP Δ - Holding Shame Proudly/Grandma Loves Grandchild.

She held shame for placing my uncle and Mother in boarding school. They were physically, emotionally, and mentally abused there. She owned a wounded child in her adult years. She lived to be one hundred and eight but never apologized for her mistakes.

I had a feeling she would pass away at this age. One hundred and eight has a lot of meanings in different cultures. One hundred and eight energy lines converge to form our heart chakra. One energy line leads to the crown chakra and it is the path to our transcending. Many world religions own routines of performing one hundred and eight daily prayers.

THIS IS CAR NUMBER 108

Do you know anyone owning shame for old mistakes?
What tools could they own to avoid shame and own apology?

TIP Δ - Abusive Father Forgiven/Father Loves Child.

He suffered from exaggerated despair.
He owned a wounded child in the body of an adult.
He could have avoided suffering by owning stable-senses tools.
He never learned to set self-discipline to himself or others.

Do you know anyone passing down negative ancestral abuse?
What tools could they have owned to be successful?

TIP Δ - Successful Gains Lost/Grandfather Loves Grandchild.

He had financial success and then spent it all to own bankruptcy.
He suffered from exaggerated joy/despair.
He owned a wounded child in the body of an adult.
He never lived within his means or maintained a budget.

Do you know anyone owning bankruptcy?
What tools could they have owned to be successful?

TIP Δ - Unprotected Life Overwhelmed/Aunt Loves Nephew.

At one time she had a family and a successful job.
She owned a wounded child in the body of an adult.
Her last days were crying from a bed with a voice ignored.
A boogey-monster of old wounds haunted her adult years.
She overdosed on pills and died at an early age.

Do you know anyone fearing a boogey-monster of old wounds?
What tools could they own to overcome their fears?

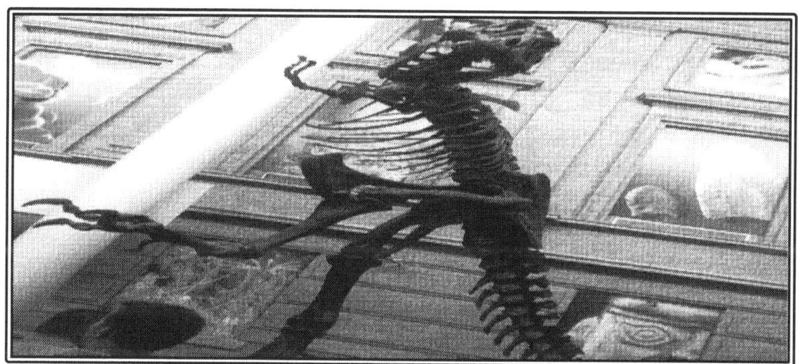

It is the day before Thanksgiving in 2010. I just completed a six-week course on how to write jokes and give successful stand-up comedy routines. My graduation present was to perform my jokes at the most well known comedy club in Atlanta Georgia. This is an excellent class and I highly recommend it. Many of the jokes in this diary are from my comedy routine.

One of the jokes I said on stage is, "I have been in therapy for damn near thirty years." "By the time I reach fifty I will be happy but homeless." I never imagined in a million years how close to reality this joke would become. The time I was on stage I was flush financially. I had tens of thousands in savings with no debt. I learned how quickly all those savings can vanish. I hadn't had debt in over twenty years.

I heard stories of famous ball players and actors who blew threw this kind of money yet I never thought it could happen to me. Yes it happened. This is real, it can happen to anyone, and it does occur. I take this as a crucial lessons learned. It is a lesson, which happened in my ancestral inheritance as well.

TIP Δ - Potential To Homeless/Uncle Loves Nephew.

At one time he had a family and a successful job.
He spent much of his life bankrupt and running from creditors.
He was a wounded child in the body of an adult.
His final days were spent crying in a homeless shelter.

Do you know anyone with potential who ended up homeless?
What tools could they have owned to be successful?

My ancestors lacked healing tools. I wish they had not blocked their transcending light journey. What would you write in your diary about your ancestors?

TIP Δ - Beyond Rock Bottom and Brother Loves Brother.

Intervention saved him from a lifetime of substance abuse.

Do you know anyone needing an intervention?
What tools could they have owned to be more successful?

TIP Δ - Hero Running Success and Brother Loves Brother.

At eighteen he left home to move to a far away location.
He cut his past so he could focus solely on the present.
He became successful due to his geographical relocation.

Do you know anyone who had to leave home to be a success?
Sometimes taking the sidewalk for geographical relocation is healing.

TIP Δ - Hurt Hero Overcomes and Brother Loves Brother.

He did vision correcting eye surgery, causing permanent eye damage.
He owned strong thoughts of suicide from constant eye pain.
His family saved him and taught him to never-give-up!

Do you know anyone overcoming a botched surgery?
What would you write in your diary about this?

I am the youngest of four brothers. As an adult, I know each sibling had to leave home to start his life. My siblings were the glue keeping my inner-self light bulb at positive vibrations. As each one left home my inner-self bulb grew dimmer and dimmer. At age of twelve they were all gone leaving me to face Angry Mother Forgiven and Abusive Father Forgiven alone. My inner-self light bulb went into an off position for quite some time.

I had to learn how to own a safe inner-self home with my loving inner-self woman and inner-self man. This is how I can own a bright future grounded in happiness and success. This picture was taken at a beautiful Denver, Colorado Christmas parade.

TIP Δ - The following are eastern/western first nation-healing.

Holistic approaches to stability, exercises, nature, and therapy.
Holistic approaches to transcending light vibrations healing.
Holistic approaches to massage, tai chi, and acupuncture.
Holistic approaches to meditation and prayer.

I unleash first-nation healing!

In computer terms, the number one refers to turning on a hardware switch and the number zero is when a hardware switch is turned off. Computer hardware runs on software. Software runs hardware based on a series of ones and zeroes.

I believe human life is one for alive or turned on.
I believe human death is zero or turned off.
Ones and zeroes are ancestors living, dying, and reincarnating.

These (0) and (1) strings create each unique transcending journey. These strings guide where I am today and in the future. These strings guide where humanity is today and in the future. I benefit from positive ancestral messages. My journey is (0) plus (1).

TIP Δ - Life on and death off are life is transcending truths. People come into and out of humanity. Step carefully.

TIP Δ - First nation-healing heals an inner-self team.
TIP Δ - First nation-healing focuses on positive ancestral messages.

Collective first nation-healing attaches to our inner-self love and transcending light vibrations. I believe inside any light from any source lives our ancestors. Our transcending equality template strings of ones and zeros are updated through every life and death.

TIP Δ - Our ancestors help us transcend birth, life, and death.
TIP Δ – While sleeping I reunite with all humanity ancestors.

First nation-healing existed upon this earth for thousands of years. The year 201 ॐ invokes first-nation healing. First nation-healing worships all of my six senses. First nation-healing consultation of transcending light vibrations, nature, and humanity is helping all of us heal.

TIP Δ - I let negative ancestral inheritance messages fade away.

TIP Δ - First nation-ancestors helped me complete this diary.

TIP Δ - First nation-healing owns no judgment, shame, or blame.

TIP Δ - Each individual humanity story is a classic collector's item.

Abusive and self-abusive messages can be passed from one generation to the next. Abusive Father Forgiven suffered instability, negative ancestral messages, and never healed his old wounds.

TIP Δ - I heal my inner-self team reminding me of my ancestors.

My transcending light quest in New York City had me going to Emergency Rooms to move beyond my break up with Hyper-Love Forgiven. I was suffering from bleeding ulcers and brain instability. I needed the ER to give me medications to own stability once again. At times, my transcending light quest went under water.

These New York City signs became all too familiar to me.

Healing education and tools could have helped me. Everyone can be inner-self aware of my personal story soon unfolding. As I describe my baby toddler years, more of my ancestral inheritance is revealed. I learn the importance to overcome inner-self team instability. I listen to 3-voice now heard messages from stability-healing heroes.

Understanding the dynamics of my household shows my foundations in fear and lack of set self-discipline.

I entered life womb-healed.
My journey survived a storm sewer of crisis.

I exist together in humanity owning I did everything for healing others and myself. My unique transcending journey is a road enlightened with inner-self transcending. Streets are paved with ancestral light helping me heal old wounds.

A great 3 came into my transcending light quest.

I learn to own the healing entrance working best for me.

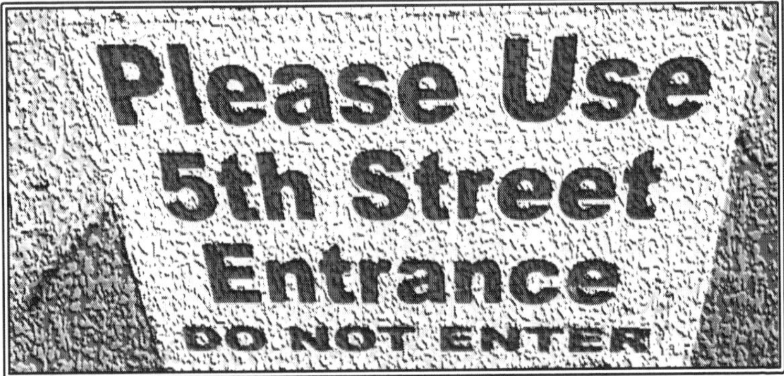

This is a picture of another transcending trail I had to walk.

Stability-Healing Questions

How does writing down MHC ancestral stories help heal?

How does writing down ancestral flaws help heal MHC?

What positive and negative ancestral messages does MHC get?

How does MHC own inner-self love?

How does MHC own inner-self playful?

How does MHC own voice now heard?

How does MHC own inner-self woman?

How does MHC own inner-self man?

How does MHC own inner-self forgiven?

How does MHC own others-self forgiven?

How does MHC own my human compassion?

How does MHC own inner-self protected?

How does MHC own voice now validated?

How does MHC own compassion-based parent?

How does MHC own inner-self transcending?

Chapter 7 Inner-Self Love

Dangerous Pangaea Danny!
Amazingly Beautiful Sunsets
Glorious Clear Night
Most Amazing Time
Photographers Truly Capture
Transcending Light Vibrations
Golden Born Tapestries
Amazing Hues Of
Smeared Ever Emboldened
Flumes Effervescent Amber
Greys Swirled White
Orange Bold Yellow
Neon Pinks Reds
Sky Blooming Nuances
Unimaginable Beauty Beholden
Glowing Amongst Earth!

I am in the kitchen and my father – Abusive Father Forgiven is pacing back and forth. Hyper energy courses throughout his body. He picks up dishes and glasses smashing them against walls. He throws dinner plates at my mother. He belts back another swig of whiskey while grumbling garbled words. He yells out in paranoid pain, "Everyone is out to get me!" He owns chaos and crisis.

Crisis owns my family.

My father's actions were no longer under his ownership. He owned brain instability. My family survived crisis. This is my most important lesson learned.

As my father paced back and forth I owned terror. I was afraid to go to the bathroom so I peed in my bed. I was screamed at for wetting the bed. I internalized I had no right to own any needs. My inability to own needs caused me to own shame and a loss of my inner-self love.

I yearned to have the loving families I saw on TV.

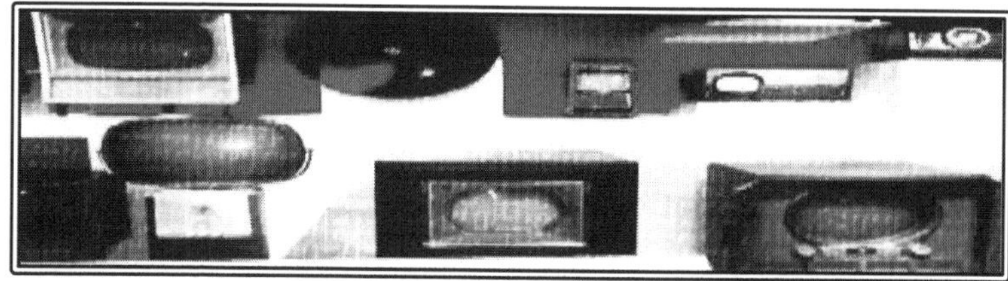

During my toddler years, I learned to silence my voice. I believed I needed to own a silent voice to survive. I watched 1970s TV shows dreaming of the family I needed. TV had the nurturing families I dreamed of. In these days, I could have used a lot more time in the great outdoors.

I took this picture at the top of Mount Elbert on my quest. This is one of many beautiful views I encountered while in Colorado.

I never saw ideal TV families acting out in crisis or hitting each other. Some TV parents allow their children a voice now heard and inner-self love. The huge costs of divorce and bankruptcy are avoided when every individual transcends to own inner-self love.

Every human on earth is a loved tribal family member of humanity. This is a picture of me with the inner-self team and family on it. I am at the top of the north rim of the Grand Canyon Arizona.

Set self-discipline keeps my transcending journey on track.

    During my transcending light quest, I lived in a loft in south Atlanta Georgia. Just outside the loft, trains were left parked there for days at a time. This is a picture of a train I had to crawl under in order to get on public transportation and complete this diary. I miss this community of diverse, artistic, and compassionate people. Some of our conversations sparked new ideas for my diary. Here is where I got graphic help putting my words on my pictures used in the cover.

I Never-Give-Up!

I own tremendous compassion for anyone entering a life of crisis to survive and prosper. I lost count of how many times I fell down and managed to get up.

Reading took me to foreign lands and adventures. I read tales of loving parents I yearned to have. Within the written word, I gained wisdom and adventure. Reading these nurturing strings of words helped give me the ideals of how to own inner-self love. Reading of inspiration and positivity helps me hold on to faith.

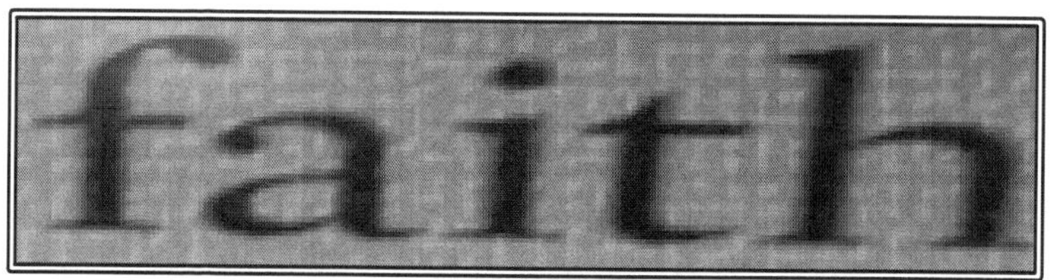

As I write this chapter, I am screaming as loud as I can. This time in my transcending I am forced into crisis. I need my inner-self child to cling to something beautiful. Is there something wonderful for me? Abusive Father Forgiven refused to own a stable well-being.

Is Abusive Father Forgiven stable or unstable today? My family never knew the current well-being of my father. No one in my family could stabilize my father. I had a toy gorilla giving me the nurturing love my parents could not. A boogey-monster existed behind every door, under every bed, and in the closet.

During these years, I did not know how to own my needs. I feared Abusive Father Forgiven and Angry Mother Forgiven. My initial transcending began in the 1970s. This was a time when there were far less healing options than there are today. Each chapter owns my child-adult-parent transcending light journey. My inner-self team manages my healing goals.

TIP Δ – Positive results evolve from the actions I take.
TIP Δ – I stop rejecting myself and I start believing in myself.
TIP Δ – I write down passions I need to bring into reality.

Instead of anger, I turn to compassion for owning my needs. I protect myself from abuse and self-abuse.

In my past, I failed to own inner-self love. I had not known myself for quite some time. I did not yet know how to own stability, how my life needs to be, and what trails I must take.

My transcending light quest reminds me of this picture. I thought I hiked randomly but it turned out to be Angel lead. I learned what I needed to complete this diary and make it as perfect as it can be. This is a picture of a map area I hiked through while I was in Phoenix, Arizona.

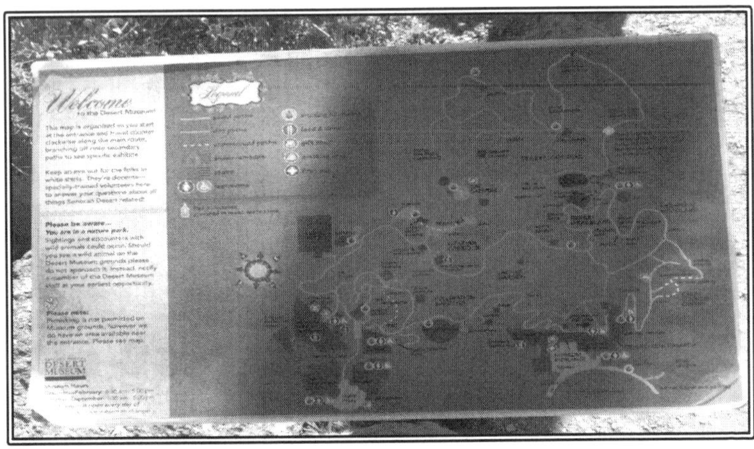

A true leader for all ages creates work and charity for the betterment of Pangaea. In this leadership role, a person becomes timeless, shapeless, and genderless. My Human Compassion is here to help create Pangaea charities.

I used to see an outwardly beautiful woman and think I need to spend time with her. I used to see an outwardly beautiful man and think I need to have his life. I learned that I am one with the same transcending light vibrations that outwardly beautiful people own.

The more I am myself the more I am not attached to anything. When I play myself in life I do not need to be anyone but me. The more I am myself and not playing false stories of old wounds the more I own healed.

TIP Δ – It's vital to own inner-self love.
TIP Δ – It's vital to own transcending light vibrations love.

I created 3-based healing ceremonies in Chapter 18. This is a picture of a 333 price I saw at a grocery store in Aurora, Colorado. At this bin they were selling candies.

This is the symbol of set self-discipline extinguishing crisis.

TIP Δ – I hear complaining and I ignore his or her complaints.

TIP Δ – I do not say anything back to a complainer.

TIP Δ – Complaining is my "love & light" reminder to be thankful.

TIP Δ – In every breath I say, "I am thankful. I am loved."

Healing is learning how to own love. Healers helped guide my quest into owning new tools to promote inner-self love.

There are unlimited transcending light vibrations to go around. Increasing world populations are not an issue. We have the wealth, resources, and food to support unlimited people. Humanity will soon start to settle other planets. The rapid advancements of technology and science make this a reality.

Have you all noticed how everything is smart? We have smart water, smart phones, and we even have smart cars! What I need to know is when did all my stuff get smarter than me?

TIP Δ – The following allows me to own inner-self love.

I get to know my inner-self team and daily well-being. I come to terms with my negative ancestry and leave it behind. I own available healing tools and healing education. I am committed to healing.

TIP Δ – I am very thankful for what I have and the needs I own.
TIP Δ – I am not thinking about what I do not have.

I transcend my voice now heard to own a voice now validated. I use my voice to own my needs. This bridge joins New York City to a borough. This is an awareness bridge symbol of transcending light vibrations and inner-self love attachments to my child-adult-parent.

TIP Δ - Every negative or positive routine has a reason behind
TIP Δ - I must understand why I am doing my actions and routines.
TIP Δ - I must adopt positive actions and routines.
TIP Δ - I write my actions and routines in my diary.

I learned to hate the smell of alcohol on my father and brother. Substance abuse prevented them from owning now. When I was born my Father owned a major mid-life crisis.

TIP Δ – Mid-life change is scary yet it also owns opportunity.
TIP Δ – Mid-life is a time when a new journey can be owned.

Stability-healing heroes help teach me to support my needs.

I replace anger with compassion. I observe and stabilize my being. I own healing tools to achieve a stable well-being.
It's a 201 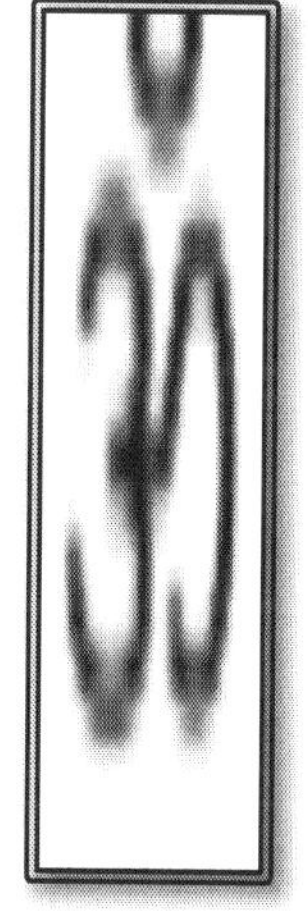 happy new year when I own stability.

I must set self-discipline and express my voice now heard for owning my needs. I am doing the best I can to compassion-based parent myself. If I take actions against my core values I suffer. In every relationship I set core values and set self-discipline.

My low self-esteem and instability are intensified when I cannot set self-discipline with others or myself. I become dependent on others for deciding my destiny. I rely on aggressive, unprotected, and or external influences to determine my journey.

TIP Δ – I am completely responsible for how my life is now.

TIP Δ – I am completely responsible for how my life turns out.

TIP Δ – I own my flaws, mistakes, and good times in the future.

This is a picture of a window I came across in Midtown Atlanta Georgia. There is a coffee shop near here where I spent a lot of time creating this diary.

My unprotected inner-self team allowed domination by others. I relied on the approval of others and feared their rejections.

TIP Δ – I own awareness of what I have been through.

TIP Δ – I own awareness of where I am.

TIP Δ – I own awareness of where I am going.

TIP Δ – I am the only one who defines my inner-self team.

TIP Δ – I am the only one who creates my inner-self home.

I am lifted up through transcending light vibrations! It takes honest courageous work to heal. I heal my 333 = ॐ ॐ ॐ

inner-self temple. I took the following picture of my shadow aura at a New York City Times Square construction sign.

I learn to inner-self pray/meditate to 333-333-3333 of inner-self love, humanity, and transcending light vibrations. This looking glass shatters the old wounded and blurry machine I used to live inside.

The 911 terrors had humanity lose child-like trust. The building of a 119-fearlessness New York City freedom tower owns 3 = ॐ compassion-based honest courageous work rising out of chaos ashes.

Out of chaos emerges our 3 universal humanity compassion. I team my AUM cord together with humanity to heal.

When I avoided stable-senses tools I got lost on my journey. Fight or flight responses are part of being human. These responses kept our ancestors alive through wars and natural disasters. It is exaggerated fight or flight that can bring crisis. When I own my stable-senses tools I bring fight or flight under my set self-discipline.

Stability-Healing Questions

Why does owning needs cause trouble for MHC?

Why must MHC forgive?

How did a silent and voice ignored halt the transcending of MHC?

How can transcending help MHC move past crisis?

What must MHC set in every relationship?

How do transcending light vibrations heal MHC?

How does inner-self love heal MHC?

What types of awareness must MHC own?

Who is responsible for how the life of MHC turns out?

What diary routines does MHC need to write in the diary?

How does writing and learning heal MHC?

How does MHC define leadership?

How do the passions of MHC heal?

Why does the teaming of MHC AUM cord with humanity help heal?

Chapter 8 Stable-Senses Tools

Tools Educated Danny
Senses Govern Moods
Ernest Hemingway Demonstrated
Exaggerated Action Adventures
Embracing Fearlessness Wow
Humans Battling Humans!
Humans Combatting Nature!
Fight or Flight?
Insatiable Exaggerated Miseries
Legendary Life Lived
Risky Negative Actions
Suffering Old Wounds
A Life Admired
But Missing Ingredients
Needing To Learn
Observed Stabilized Moods
Safety, acceptance, and stability
Inner-Self Love

It is my view the author Ernest Hemingway suffered from brain instability. His substance abuse made things worse. After reading his biography I see his old ancestral wounds in the bowels of his soul. His negative actions put him and his family in grave danger.

TIP Δ – Crisis and chaos are slavery to routines owning suffering.
TIP Δ – I can choose crisis or stability.

Hemingway intentionally owned crisis. His outer life owned legend yet its roots owned vast sufferings.

Creative people might believe substance abuse, avoiding needs, and purposely owning a crisis filled life increases creativity. I believe creative people achieve vastly improved creations if they own stability, avoid addictions, and prevent all forms of abuse.

Owning stable-senses tools gives me positive stops on my journey. The following picture is a frequent stop I made on A New York City subway.

I have been lost to the addiction to negative thoughts in my head. My repetitive negative judgments hurt me. I become aware of this and it is just the false illusion story I have told myself about myself. My past has no power over me. My awareness comes when I own this looking glass shattered reality.

Stable-senses tools have increased my creative abilities while removing anxiety, instability, and crisis. This in turn allows me to own my stability and needs.

When I owned despair everything in my life was hopeless. I spent too much time without ambition. I owned exaggerated and seemingly constant inner-self chatter without being able to have a love attachment with our divine. I thought everything would go my way even though I was not prepared for it.

TIP Δ – Everyone can own positive or negative routines.

Should I withdraw cash from an ATM after dark (negative)?
Should I withdraw cash from an ATM during daylight (positive)?

TIP Δ – I evaluate if my current actions are positive or negative.
TIP Δ – I write these actions into my diary.

Stable-senses tools allow me to be my own best friend forever!

TIP Δ – The following own my positive actions.

Compassion-based listening.
Communicating with well-being available talking.
Choosing positive relationships with stability-healing heroes.

A person who is abusive might put on a false act. Eventually their abusive tendencies show. I watch their actions and own immediate action if abuse appears. My life is far to precious to own negative actions. I cut negative umbilical cords.

TIP Δ – I evaluate any relationship while using these principles:

I avoid partners putting me down verbally or calling me names.
I avoid partners who do not allow me a voice now heard.
I avoid relationships when mutual needs are not shared.
I avoid relationships if my core values do not agree with theirs.
I do not enter relationships lacking stability.

TIP Δ – I cut cords lacking mutual well-being availability.

I own needs and stability. I observe and stabilize my well-being. I learn and avoid all toxins, foods, environments, and people I am allergic to. I own honesty with healers. I own inner-self meditation and inner-self prayer.

TIP Δ –I cut and attach the umbilical cord relationships working best for me. I am my best inner-self crime prevention unit.

Crime Prevention Unit

Abusive Father Forgiven never listened to any voice but his own. If a person doesn't allow my set self-discipline, I get away. I take time with relationships and don't rush into anything. If a person continually talks over me, I cut my cord with them. I figure out if a person is abusive to themselves or others. I learn my partner's negative ancestral inheritance.

One of my most important childhood memories was a particular day at Kindergarten in the early 1970s. I was five years old and while swinging on the swing set I had diarrhea. I felt shame my parents or friends would find out so I decided not to tell anyone. I spent the entire day with diarrhea in my pants. I rode the school bus home ashamed of my inner-self team. I thought the teacher would yell at me if I asked for getting my needs met of clean clothes and a shower. Sitting in diarrhea is a symbol of my inability to own needs.

I owned ancestral messages passed down into my youth; I must sit in my human waste rather than ask for help. I used to hold my inner-self team to blame for my painful life.

My needs and my voice were not worthy of being heard. I did not deserve to own help, have help, or seek help. The needs of others took priority over mine. While owning instability any perception of abuse or danger (actual or not) caused me to own exaggerated fight or flight whose side affects are anxiety, fear, and inflammation. I owned bleeding ulcers and an inability to own a proper night's sleep. I owned nervous shaking hands.

When I faced troubles, no matter how small, I felt the need to own exaggerated fight or flight.
Unstable fight or flight owned fireworks for my inner-self team.

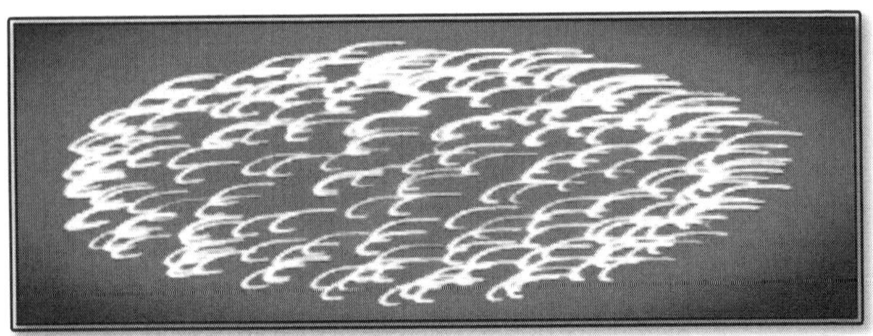

TIP Δ - These following helps me own an aware inner-self team:

I own full breathes getting me through stress, conflict, and crisis. I am well-being available with my trusted healers. I write daily well-being into my diary so I may own beautiful 333 transcending.

I took the following picture at a New York City Museum of Art. This is an ancient Asian statue that symbolizes stability.

It is my non-clinical view that famous authors, musician, actors, and other creative talents die prematurely due to well-being instability. I believe the risk portions of the brain are not fully developed until we are in our early thirties. I also believe distinct ages in life are more likely to own instability. In my own life the ages of around fourteen, twenty-eight, and forty-two owned greater instability. I have known many who owned drug overdose and suicide at or around those ages.

TIP Δ - I overcame fear to embrace healing.
TIP Δ - I am free to own present day living.

I stayed at many healing hostels on my transcending light quest. These stays were critical for the completion of this diary and vital for my own healing. My stability-healing diary reveals a reflection of myself during my unique transcending journey. I write in my diary where I am. I stay in open hostels across the country to remind me I am never alone. I took this photo at a hostel in Phoenix Arizona.

I waited on the Metro light rail in Phoenix, Arizona at 6:33pm and I ordered a meal in Phoenix and the bill was $6.33. I came across so many threes. The number three inspired my writings.

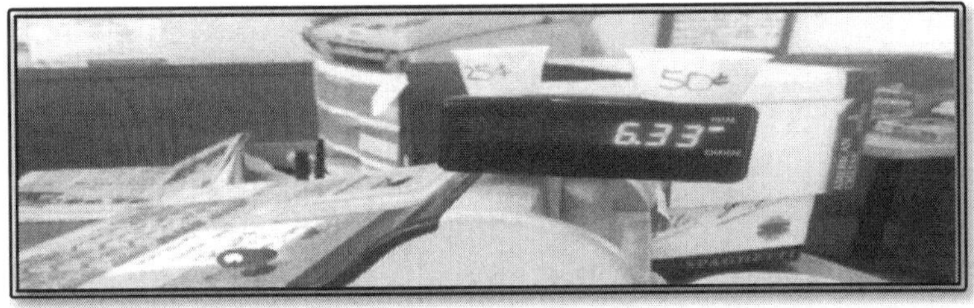

What occurred in my family represents negative ancestral inheritance. Suicide, substance abuse, poverty, homelessness, jail, and bankruptcy lead to crisis passed from one generation to the next.

TIP Δ - Humanity is here to provide compassion to all.
TIP Δ - Humanity owns human civil rights.

I took this picture before hiking a trail in the Rocky Mountains Colorado. Individual Pangaea trail suffering unites us all.

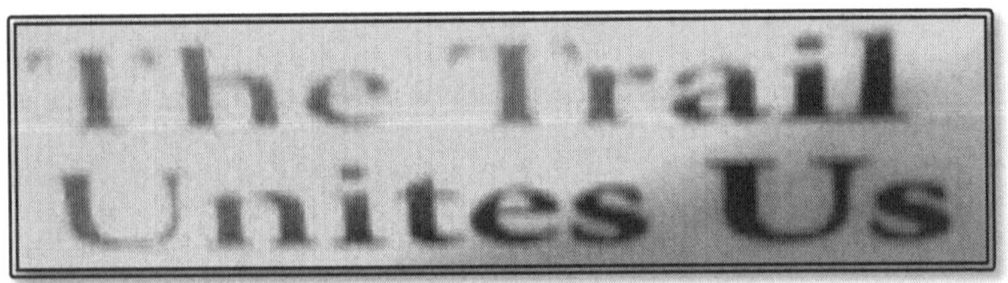

When I heal my inner-self team, I am healing humanity. My journey steps are headed up to healing. I took these same steps to hike out of a New York City subway.

I light ancestral healing candles to help me heal. I light ancestral healing candles to heal humanity. This photo of memorial candles was taken at the Spanish mission near Tucson Arizona.

Freedom is the time after birth when I am free to own play. I run through fields of grass over my head alive-owning-now. Using child-like imagination I become a fish owning no worries.

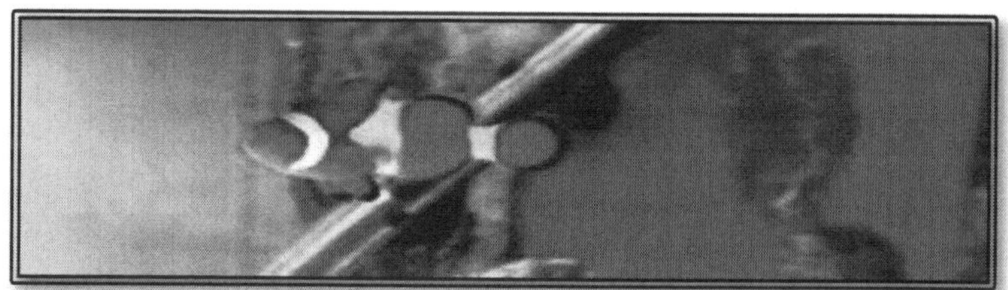

Nature and its beautiful visuals and music heal me. This picture was taken on a hike in the Appalachian Trails of northern Georgia.

I hiked in Canyon lands Utah with both arms. I was Utah prepared! I made sure and went with friends through the slot canyons and they helped guide me on my journey so I didn't lose an arm.

TIP Δ - I could own my old wounds into my retirement years.

Early childhood traumatic overwhelmed my adult years. My physical body aged beyond the age of twelve, yet my well-being still owned the age of twelve when my trauma first occurred.

I view seagulls flying and use my imagination to see all of my negative ancestral messages on the tips of their wings. These beautiful birds magically take my old wounds into transcending light vibrations so they permanently fade away. I took this picture of seagulls flying over me while at Coney Island in New York City.

I can now view all of our shared ancestors, God, and Humanity living inside any source of light I might encounter. This light was taken at a park in Atlanta, Georgia.

I read through any religious text from all known religions, spirituality, teachers, and gurus. I replace any word refering to a type of God or any type of Prophet with the word Humanity. It is amazing how that text reads now! This is so amazingly incredible!

TIP Δ – I read through all known religious texts and replace anywhere that it says God or Prophet with the name – Humanity!

I transcend to heal old wounds. I move my inner-self team to inner-self protected and I overcame negative risk taking.

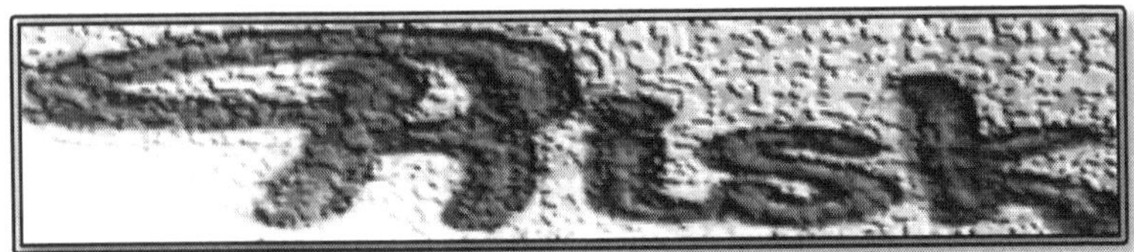

My inner-self team learned how to cry and I am better for that. Owning inner-self protected disrupts my dangerous out-of-order ancestry so I can heal. I am authorized to own my set self-discipline privacy on my unique transcending journey.

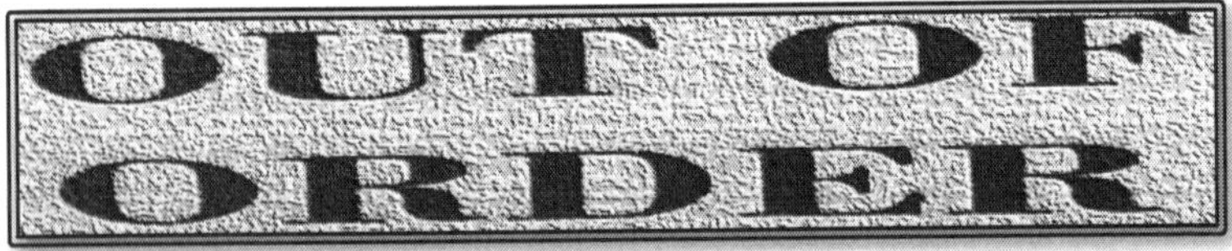

I hike my transcending light quest with all my possessions in one bag. I pause to breathe in the glorious healing that nature provides.

What would be in your transcending light quest backpack?

TIP Δ - I can say, "I love you" to another person without judgment.
TIP Δ - I can say, "I need help" to stability-healing heroes.
TIP Δ - I no longer fear change, death, living, or the unknown.
TIP Δ - I own stable-senses tools and positive actions to heal.
TIP Δ - I reach rock bottom every day and rise up from there!

The hands of humanity hold 119-fearlessness.

I make Pangaea a more compassionate healed place. Peace, enlightenment, and equal feminine/masculine are spread everywhere.

A boogey-monster existed in my home, under every bed, and in my room. This monster reaches up in attempts to violate my inner-self team and destroy my set-self discipline. I know my boogey-monster fears but I don't own them. I own inner-self protected so my inner-self boogey-monster disappears. I refuse to own scared on my journey!

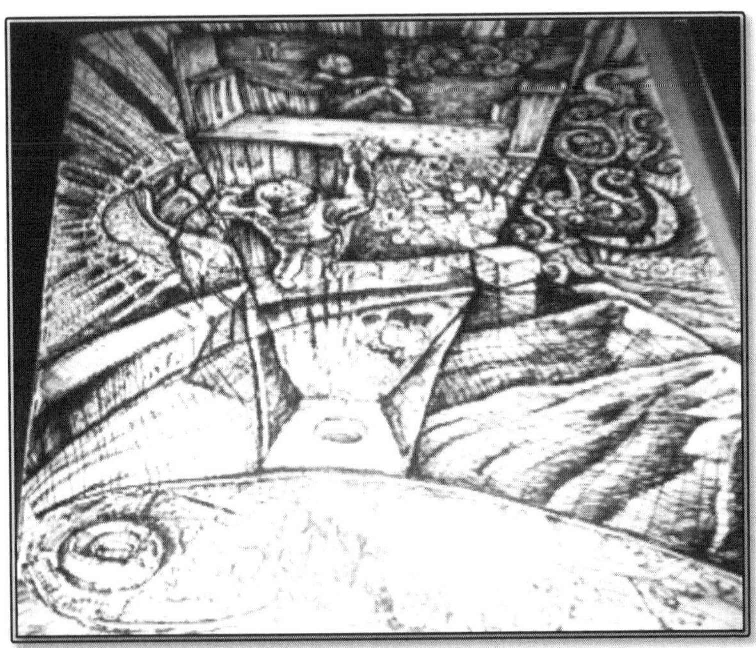

The art shown above is by Steven Thompson mcdurphurp@gmail.com.
His username is TranceParadox and website http://stproductions.snappages.com.

Stability-Healing Questions

How does owning positive actions help heal MHC?

What are the unique ways MHC uses to own stability?

How are negative actions affecting MHC?

How does owning awareness help heal MHC?

How can MHC identify an abusive person?

Who are the partners MHC must avoid?

What are the MHC descriptions of a stable partner?

How does the MHC metaphorical sitting in waste apply to needs?

What is in the MHC transcending light quest backpack?

How does exaggerated fight or flight affect MHC?

How can MHC disrupt negative ancestral messages?

How does ancestral light help heal MHC?

How can Pangaea trails unite and heal us all?

How does 119-fearlessness heal MHC?

Chapter 9 Inner-Self Protected

Crisis Protected Danny
Now Life Owned
Womb-Healed Forever
Seek Fulfill Own
Compassion-Based Parent
Forever Loving My
Inner-Self Child
Human Civil Rights
Freedom Owning Needs
Safety, acceptance, and stability
Inner-Self Protected
119-Fearlessness Cherished
Transcending Every Day!
From First Walk
Healed Happy Baby
Child-Like Trust
Goes Forth Now
Never-Give-Up!

When I was seven, Abusive Father Forgiven was in the kitchen. It was snowing out. He threw pots and dishes around. He said to me, "Son, I work all day doing research with technical lab equipment. Everything in my job has order and I kept this job for way too many years. I compute precise calculations and exact measurements. My work demands stability. I am throwing these pots and pans around to own crisis and teach you that chaos is positive!"

Owning crisis and chaos were tattooed upon me as a positive.

Crisis was déjà vu for my family. I had taken a front seat looking glass view in my Danny years. Abusive Father Forgiven grabbed kitchen items from cupboards and violently threw them. Some landed on the ceiling and others on the walls. He screamed in a twisted blend of exaggerated joy and pain. My father desperately needed to own stability.

Deep down abusive father forgiven showed illness from negative ancestral history and life trauma. He owned a wounded inner-self child lashing out. His unstable brain fueled his adult child-like temper tantrums.

Abusive Father Forgiven told me about his experiences as an army private during the Korean War. It is in the early nineteen-fifties. He was stationed at a chemical core in Utah. He created deadly biological weapons. While mixing toxins into canisters, he often heard loud practice drill alarms going off. These interruptions made it hard for him to hold onto these metal cylinders. There were multiple times he came close to dropping them. Had he let go instant death would have overwhelmed him.

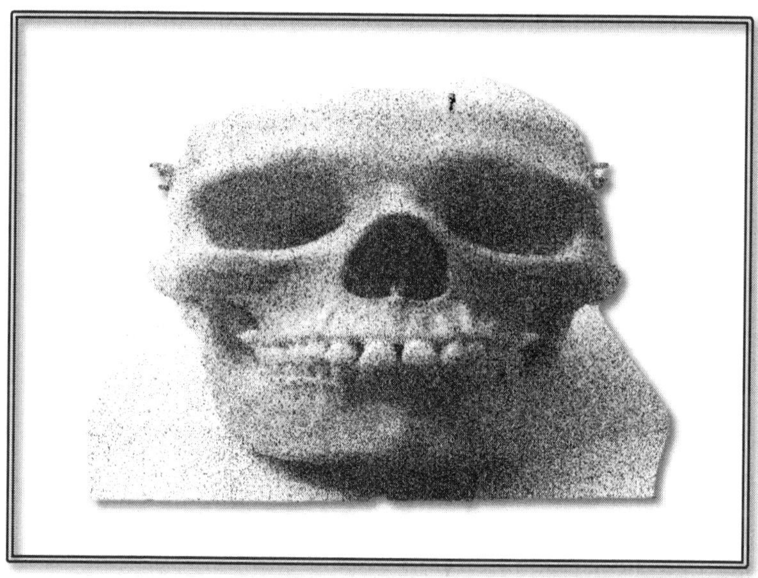

I grew up in the early seventies where many owned fears of the Soviet Union attacking us with nuclear and or biological weapons. My school had drills where I hid under a desk to own my safety. We all knew that this drill was useless. Had all out nuclear and biological war been carried out between our country and the Soviets, a small student desk would do nothing to protect me or anyone else. All of Pangaea would be annihilated.

My father owned a standard issue army knife, pipe fitters wrench, and gas mask to defend against attack. These were objects owning his defense from anyone who might break into the house and attempt to hurt him. These same items dominated my family.

The idea I had to appease my father's domination led me to owning a title of people pleaser. I was programmed since birth to help others while ignoring my needs. This led me to own difficulty in answering these questions.

What are my goals and needs?
How do I exit old wounds?

TIP Δ - I moved beyond old wounds to be alive-owning-now.
TIP Δ - I took compassion-based training to own my needs.
TIP Δ - I became responsible to own inner-self protected.

I own inner-self protected well-being surveillance.

TIP Δ - Inner-self protected allows me to own a voice now heard.

TIP Δ - I can own safety, acceptance, and stability.

In my early years, I had ancestral inheritance of new intimate umbilical cord attachments being dangerous. As I aged, I kept relationships distant. My inner-self team decides to cut or attach cord relations. The wonders of child-like trust are forever within me.

My oldest brother, Beyond Rock Bottom, left home shortly after I turned seven. He graduated from high school to start his new life. As an adult, I know why my siblings left. As a child, it felt as if my favorite dog left me at a Christmas parade in Denver, Colorado.

Why was I left all alone with Angry Mother Forgiven?
Why was I left all alone with Abusive Father Forgiven?

At the age of nine, I went into the kitchen and put a pot on my head. I walked into the living room to be with my parents. I danced around attempting to own laughter yet no one laughed. My parents yelled at me to leave. I owned shame and rejection. My inner-self light bulb grew dimmer and my self-esteem plummeted. I had a voice attempting to own laughter to anyone owning despair. This defining event encouraged me to become a comedian and author.

At their core, my parents were not that different. They both spent their lives in the area of healing. My Mother saved many lives with her non-profit teaching people the tools to overcome substance abuse and get back to work. My Father spent his life doing research to cure cancer. Some of his published research papers have been used to create new medications for curing cancer. These are positive influences for me to become a healer.

TIP Δ - I could have spent my entire lifetime owning old wounds.

At thirteen, puberty came. I transformed into a man while becoming more unprotected and shy. I quit my hobbies. My inner-self light bulb got dimmer as I owned despair.

I had not yet learned how to own inner-self protected. My parenting was through television shows including *Gilligan's Island* and the *Partridge Family*. All of my brothers had now left home. My inner-self team light bulb became very dim. Who am I?

Where is my journey going?

I kept my body unstable by eating inflammatory junk foods. My inner-self team senses instability would carry on into adult years. Oh I miss my inner-self child Danny. I miss Danny so much!

I Never-Give-Up!

My inner-self team is here to heal, protect me, and avoid crisis. There is always hope in any situation no matter how chaotic. My never-give-up approaches replace crisis with stability.

TIP Δ – There is a way out of instability a new healed day will come.
TIP Δ – I must own healing tools and education to own my stability.

I owned instability by putting either myself on an exaggerated pedestal or putting others on an exaggerated pedestal.

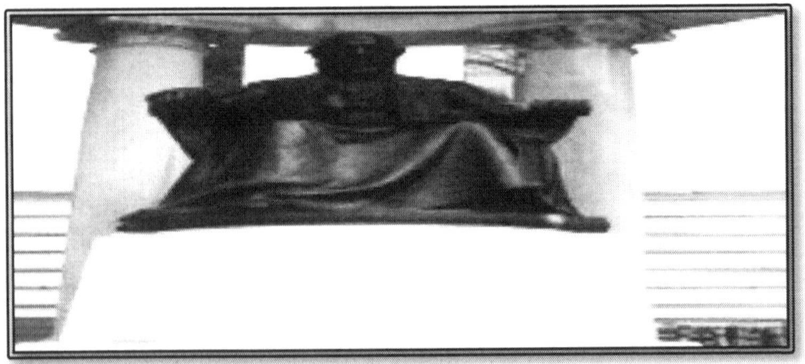

TIP Δ – No human is ever on a pedestal.
TIP Δ – Everyone owns beautiful flaws enrolling us into humanity.

I vote yes for 3-compassion-based quest roadwork to healing. The future starts here.

These following are good parts of my Father's teachings.

My Father taught me the crucial importance of learning. He encouraged healing through our wonders of nature. We shared healing hikes in nature, travel, listening to music, and zoo visits.

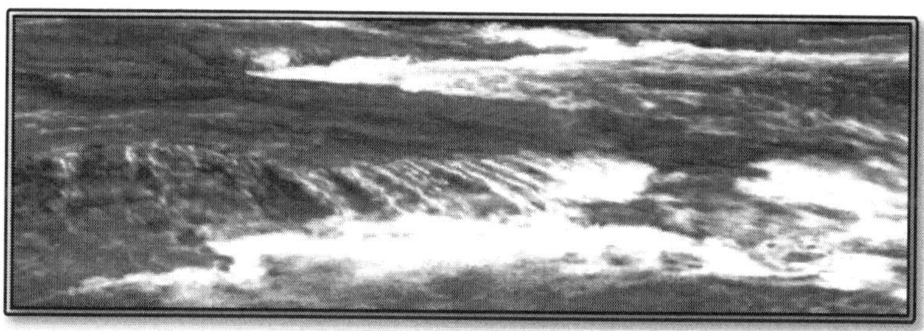

TIP Δ – Nature images, sound, taste, touch, and smell own stability.

TIP Δ – During trauma, I recall my womb-healing to own stability.

My father never owned crisis while in nature. I camp, hike, swim, and ride bikes. I focus my now on a flowing stream. I sit silently and comfortably outdoors while meditating and praying. I breathe in while focusing on my breathing inhalation and exhalation.

TIP Δ – Nature forbids me from owning fantasy.

TIP Δ – Stress/anxiety vanish when enjoying nature and the now.

This is a picture of the wilderness where my transcending light quest began. In 2010 I began writing this diary and in 2011, I started randomly hiking the Appalachian Trail and the cities of the northeastern areas of the country.

I consider the major cities in these regions including Atlanta GA, Richmond, VA, Washington D.C, New York City, and Boston MA, and Portland ME to be part of the Appalachian Trail.

It was not long ago when all of these areas were covered with forests and vegetation. It was the same ice age extending from Canada down to Georgia that created the Appalachian Mountains we know today. These mountains were carved out the land where these major cities reside. This is why I believe I finished all 2100 miles from Georgia to Maine a very unique way. Alternating between trails and cities on the Appalachian Trail is a remarkable education.

The longest stretch of the Appalachian Trails I hiked non-stop was for a consecutive two weeks. I averaged fifteen miles of hiking per day. After leaving Hot Springs North Carolina I made it north of the Damascus Virginia area. I was in Damascus for trail days. This is a huge festival with hikers and campers from around the country. It attracts around thirty thousand people every year and many vendors showcase the latest camping products.

When I was in the Boy Scouts I was involved with a lot of Appalachian Trail (AT) hiking in Tennessee and North Carolina. When I lived in Atlanta Georgia I did a lot of hiking on the AT. I have not hiked every inch of the AT in these three states however I have done a huge amount of hiking and camping there.

I remember thinking on my hikes at the start of the AT what I would encounter if I would go north of Georgia, Tennessee, and North Carolina. This is why I started out in the far north reaches of North Carolina to hike into a brand new area of southern Virginia.

I came across many through-hikers devoting anywhere from three to six months to hike the entire 2100 miles from Georgia to Maine at one consecutive time. The other types of hikers (such as myself) are called section hikers. They do entire sections at one time over a period of years and can eventually finish the entire AT hike.

I am not a veteran. I wish I had been a veteran in my earlier years. I joined fellowships of new hikers I met on trails, hostels, and supply runs. These experiences are "somewhat" like it is to be a veteran. No one was shooting at me! During my AT hike I realized that the most important charity is to help our veterans returning from war.

This is one of many Washington D.C. stops I made to own the questions, answers, and education I needed to finish this diary. I owe everything to the brave service and sacrifice of our veterans.

On my quest I heard a lot of stories about the down sizing of jobs

An empty pedestal is a symbol that no person is on any pedestal.

The goal of MHC is to make your dreams into a reality.

I once believed every person and situation must be perfect. This type of thinking caused me suffering.

TIP Δ – All people, all events, and all environments own flaws.

My fantasies imagined a super hero guarding my childhood home. When all my siblings left, I had to turn to myself to survive.

What kept me whole?
What kept me going?

In my teenage years I fell asleep with super heroes protecting me. I loved reading comic book stories. Super heroes own amazing abilities. Some make fire from their eyes, fly, or go back in time. I might not have super heroes however I do have life is transcending super heroes. The next chapter describes who these people are.

Stability-Healing Questions

Why is MHC taught that owning crisis is a positive?

What does MHC write in the diary about crisis?

If crisis calls, what steps does MHC take to own stability?

What tools heal MHC from old wounds?

What old wounds were passed down to MHC?

How do old wounds affect MHC present day living?

Why does MHC own a terrified inner-self child into adulthood?

Why would MHC want perfect people, events, and situations?

What life is transcending ways can MHC own inner-self protected?

How does MHC use nature to overcome crisis?

How does owning positives of abusive father forgiven heal MHC?

People, events, and situations are flawed; how can this heal MHC?

How does hiking the Appalachian Trail help heal MHC?

Why are Veterans the most important charity?

Chapter 10 Humanity Super Heroes

Mortality Educated Dan
Cry Danny Cry!
Yell Dan Yell!
Grief Daniel Grief!
Well-Being Transcending
Alive-Owning-Now
Today Does Own
My First Steps
Walking Beyond Despair
Safety, acceptance, and stability
Learning Educating Transcending
Journey Awakened Freedom!
Forever-Overcoming Struggle
Positive Core Values
Set Self-Discipline
Inner-Influenced Actions
Stable-Senses Tools
Courage Hope Joy
Human Civil Rights
Womb Birth Guaranteed
Needs Forever Owned

When I was sixteen, I owned instability. Everyone needed my help because of my exaggerated inner-self lacking an ability to meditate and embrace the love of our divine. I could do any job and overcome any obstacle no matter how difficult. My exaggerated inner-self abilities were far different than the unprotected person of my teenage years.

A comic book super hero is seen as role models for courage and fearlessness. Their counterpart is the monster.

When a super hero destroys a monster, a fake sense of fair pervades. Ideals of super hero "life is fair" teachings go against the life is transcending approach.

Life is transcending heroes are veterans, emergency personnel, sensory stability heroes, and stability-healing heroes.

Life is transcending heroes are beautifully human.

TIP Δ – Celebrities and royalty are no better than any of us.
TIP Δ – The more I own inner-self love the less I own old wounds.

The intimacy my parents showed each other was cord attached to negative low vibrations of anger, negative ancestral inheritance, and crisis. I trusted my parents and they let me down.

At the age of fifteen I was in the den reading magazines. I refused to wear a belt and my belly hung over my pants. I had quit all my martial arts classes, piano concerts, and Boy Scout hiking.

Why was Angry Mother Forgiven angry with me?

This misplaced anger my Mother had given me caused me to own fears that everything and everyone were out to hurt me. Exaggerated fight or flight caused me to own unrealistic approaches to living. My journey was looking glass paralyzed.

I put up a façade of a smiley happy face. I had this front so others could not see me deep down inside. I wanted this appearance so others could not notice my old wounds inside my adult body.

Unrealistic fear caused me to beware of everything. I took this photo during my quest in Atlanta Georgia.

I needed to reunite with the womb-healed relationship I once owned with my mother. I would be a rebellious teenager against my Mother well into my forties. I feared new relationships would turn into the one I had with my angry parents. I owned blues impaired despair when losing my parents to the anger of their divorce.

Angry Mother Forgiven gave me ownership of these words:

Danny! I am ashamed of you.
Danny! I demand perfection from you.
Danny! You are useless, broken, and lazy.
Danny! You are a complete failure in everything.

Abusive Father Forgiven gave me ownership of these words:

Danny! You will always follow my orders.
Danny! Your needs are nothing and my needs are everything.
Danny! I am your dictator and I will always dominate you.
Danny! You must silence your voice to survive around me.
Danny! You are only to hear what my voice needs you to do.
Danny! I will put you in a homeless shelter if you disagree with me.

After each of us is born, the messages from a Mother and father are seemingly **all powerful** from a child's point of view:

> Momma, help me?
> Daddy, help me?
> Humanity, help me?
> God, help me?

My parental messages are from negative ancestral inheritance and old wounds. These false messages had me believe I was very different from all others and unable to maintain true love. My Mother and Father said this message - "I love you only if you do what I know is right for you."

My parent's rejections of me had me falsely believe everyone should reject me. My parent's divorce and negative ancestry seeded me with old wounds lasting well into my forties. My Father metaphorically grabbed my right arm and my Mother metaphorically grabbed my left arm - ripping my inner-self child in half. This ripped up inner-self child would live the next thirty years in my adult body. Through it all our shared ancestral light shined upon me and this light reminded me to never-give-up!

I wished I were born into an orphanage so I would not have owned my parents view of how I needed to be. As an orphan I could live how our transcending light vibrations and I need to be

I made my negative history and culture fade away. One day I stepped outside a door and vowed my negative ancestry and old wounds owned no importance in present day living. This picture is in Midtown Atlanta Georgia where I worked on this diary.

Negative ancestry is how I once parented myself into my adult years. I learned to deny abusive parental messages. These negative ancestral messages said I was exaggeratingly flawed. I punished my inner-self team for very minor mistakes. If I did not create work of perfection I chastised myself that it was not good enough.

When others gave me helpful advice I viewed this as criticism. Everything I did had to be perfect. Even if it was seen as perfect, it was not good enough.

TIP Δ – Negative ancestry is not from transcending light vibrations.
TIP Δ – I forgive myself.

My diary entries uncover how I am present day parenting my inner-self child. I am careful to see if I parent myself on my parent's destructive lessons, or if I parent myself based on my positive compassion-based parenting. My negative self-parenting caused me to close down. My inner-self team wasn't sure when it was safe for me to return back into my body. I lived as a zombie. In those zombie years I really hoped I could return to live in my body.

Every day our universal transcending light vibrations have my negative ancestry fade away. My stability-healing ceremonies help in this process. My compassion-based parenting is how I open my journey once again.

My Mother showed me as much anger as one can reveal. I tried to put up a magazine to defend my inner-self team from her anger. Angry Mother Forgiven ripped it out of my hands and threw it on the floor. Her words and actions at this time wounded me for years.

"You cannot and will never flight from my blinding rage."
"You will never own set self-discipline with me."

When my Mother grabbed the magazine from my hands and threw it on the ground I felt as if I had been abused. Losing this magazine was my last line of protection from her mismanaged rage. Pangaea seemed dangerous and crisis filled. As a wounded twelve-year old, in the body of an adult, I owned I could never find a place to be home, own my needs, or own stability.

Angry Mother Forgiven told me I was a failure.
Abusive Father Forgiven taught me crisis and chaos is okay.

I used to cry and Angry Mother Forgiven said, "Stop feeling sorry for yourself!" I stopped crying and feeling alive.

Sometimes my inner-self child Danny needs to cry and own moods.

TIP Δ - When I own grief and sadness, crying helps me heal.
TIP Δ - I can cry and I am allowed to sob tears to heal grief.

At this time, my 333 inner-self team car was stolen from its parking spot. I stopped owning well-being availability.

In my attempt to avoid the hurt of old wounds I believed I owned a superior self-esteem at times. Other times I owned vast despair. Why should I bother with owning needs like paying bills or eating well? I ate fried chicken gizzards in Atlanta Georgia because they were cheap. I got oh so sick and nauseous after eating them. Never again will I eat these gizzards. I felt inner-self team shame for being unable to own my needs.

Flaws are not the traits of comic book super heroes. Pangaea cultures say suck it up and hold on to inner-self team wounds. Get over it and never cry. Society teaches us to own super strength when overcoming wounds. Strength is code word to avoid crying, avoid well-being availability, and avoid compassion-based listening.

An inability to own my needs had me own fears of a boogey-monster deep inside. I came across this bear warning sign on my hike near Veil Colorado. I see these signs and own fear.

If family, friends, or strangers hurt me I started concluding humanity is negative. I cannot generalize my personal experiences or what the media reports or my personal experiences are on how to define humanity (mostly angry or mostly compassionate). I seek humanities open hand looking glass *veritas* (truth) to answer this.

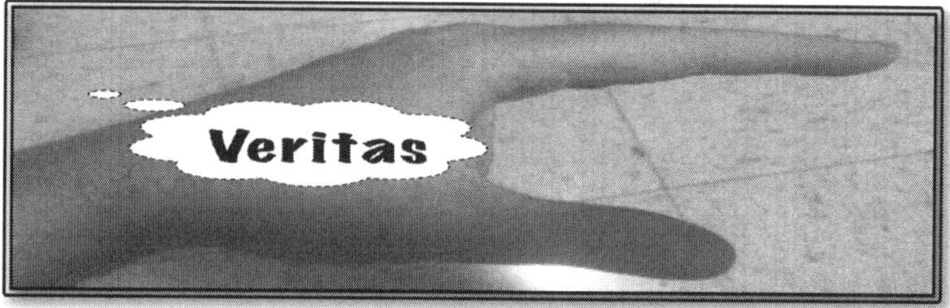

I owned fear of Abusive Father Forgiven. At times he owned anger at hearing my child-like enthusiasm for life. I loved to ask lots of questions about life, nature, and how everything works. My Father is a genius and he owned the answers for many things yet his patience was low. He had a short fuse and blew up easily.

He forced me out of the car because of my constant stream of questioning. I felt homeless, sad, and I started crying. I stopped asking questioning and my inner-self light bulb energy went dim.

At times it has been a struggle to separate present day living from old wounds. I stand up to fear to be free from old destructive influences. I do not need to own exaggerated fight or flight. I own brand new healing directions through cities and wilderness. I used this Marta train map to travel around Atlanta, Georgia.

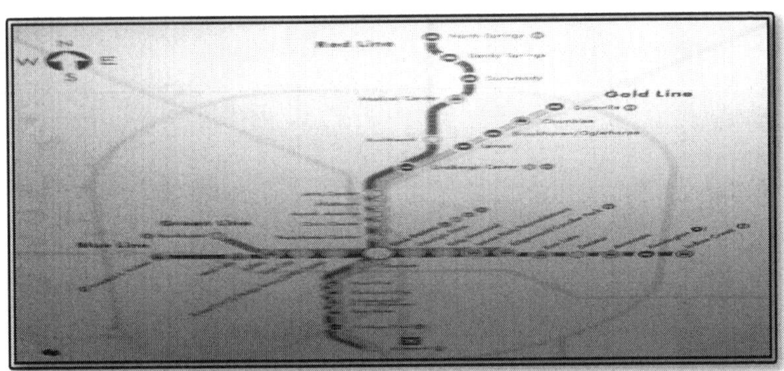

There were ancestral transfers of shame owned by my parents passed to me. I teach my inner-self team to be free of shame. It was easier for my parents to shame me rather than deal with their destructive marriage. My family was spinning out of control and Danny could do nothing to stop it.

I learned people do not always do what is in the best interest of others. Others do not do what I think they should do or what I need. People do what they need to do.

TIP Δ – I am responsible for owning my needs.

I once rejected all the parts of me reminding me of childhood. I needed to own compassion and inner-self love yet at this time I did not know how. I am my catalyst for positive changes.

TIP Δ - Inner-self parent Daniel protects inner-self child Danny.

TIP Δ - I learn to love the past, present, and future parts of myself.

I fill myself up with 333 AUM and 12 first nation-healing names.

I am not allowing old wounds to interfere with adult goals. I can express myself without fear. I overcome old wounds. I go ahead and own inner-self love because I know I want to.

Humanity super heroes protect metropolis.

I learn to forgive my ancestors, parents, siblings, and bullies. Forgiving all happening in my past allows me to own first nation-healing names inner-self forgiven and others self-forgiven. Forgiving old wounds allows me to own compassion and heal.

I am very thankful for the safety my life journey has owned. I am thankful for transcending light vibrations guidance. I took these street signs in Atlanta, Georgia. I was walking to a coffee shop to work on my diary.

I transcend my compassion. My transcending light quest owns me to new Colorado and Arizona people, stories, and places. I sold this thirty-liter backpack when leaving Colorado for Arizona. I then bought a used forty six-liter backpack so I could hold more.

After leaving my current town I would take all the clothes and items not fitting into one bag to a local thrift store or church. I love getting back down to one bag. At a new town I visit a thrift store to buy more clothes.

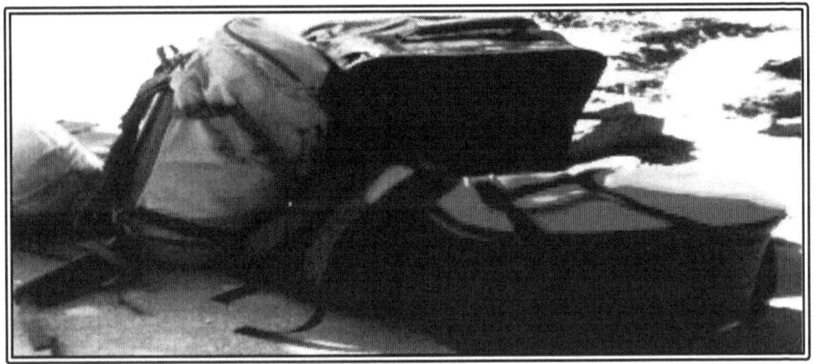

I was programmed to own life punches without asking for help. This is false. Sometimes I cannot own life alone. Current suicide rates own the importance to teaching others how to ask for help. I can say, "I need help" to my stability-healing heroes.

Strong is not the same as hiding my current well-being. I use family outings and events with my diary writings and pictures. This photo is my Mother and Father when they were first married. They did not yet have anger and old wounds. They owned so much love!

Collective humanity's compassion owns Pangaea peace. Everyone can own compassion and inner-self love to heal Pangaea. This picture showcases Pangaea birthplace of all humanity – Africa.

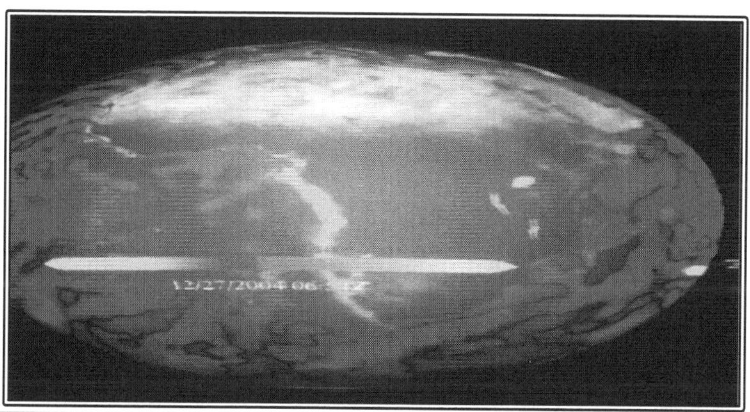

My daily routine has me texting compassion to myself. I own my 33 compassion-based healing for my inner-self team.

TIP Δ – I imagine the person I love the most. I think about my love for them and own this for myself.

TIP Δ – Wherever my airplane lands, whatever soil I hike upon, and any ocean I swim - I am always home. This is inner-self home.

The next chapter introduces the crucial importance of choosing compassion when anger rises within. I can own compassion and inner-self love to overcome any stress, crisis, and illness. I learn how to trash negative low vibrations of anger, blame, shame, guilt, judgments, external influences, inner-self chatter, and old wounds.

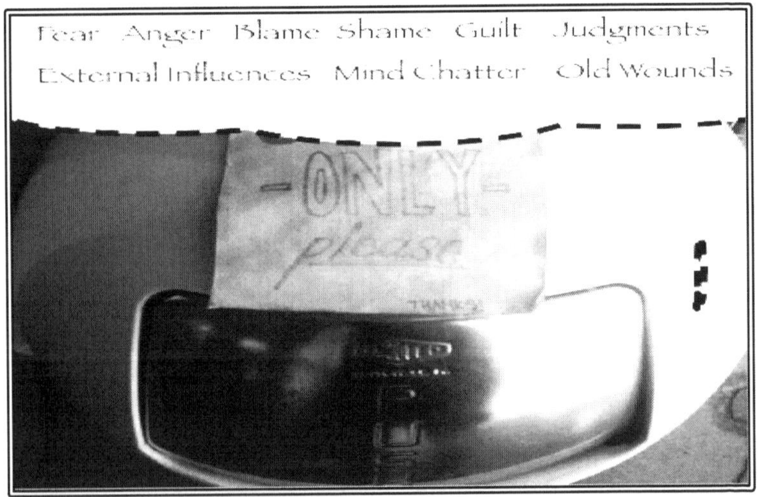

Stability-Healing Questions

How do MHC parent's messages cause old wounds?

Why did MHC feel different than others?

Why would MHC wish to be a super hero?

How does accepting humanity super heroes help heal MHC?

How does owning flaws help heal MHC?

How does crying help heal MHC?

Why does MHC eat chicken gizzards?

How does MHC stop listening to old wounds of shame?

How does MHC define life is transcending heroes?

Why does MHC rebel against his Mother for years?

How did MHC parent's divorce rip his inner-self team apart?

How does MHC overcome negative ancestral messages?

Why does MHC only want mortal pedestrian access?

What low vibrations does MHC need to throw in the trash?

Chapter 11 Anger To Compassion

Danny Owns Compassion
Stop I Yelled!
Inner-Self Agonized
Feet Faithfully Supporting
Toppled Onto Ground
Bullies Laughter Echoed
Thousands Of Feet
Kicked My Head
Angry Humanity Strangers
Pain Sliced Through
Every Body Cell
Body Shaking Carcass
Agony Owned Me
Desperately Holding Life
Inner-Self Team
Shouting Into Silence
Stop Please Stop!
Desolation Fills Soul
Is Humanity Angry?
Is Humanity Compassionate?

Every person can choose to own anger or own compassion. This decides the collective fate of humanity. I can choose to view our humanity as mostly angry or compassionate.

TIP Δ - I will not let anger affect my stability.
TIP Δ - I will not let anger lose my ability to own my needs.

There are compassionate ways I own my needs without turning to anger. I own stable-senses tools to turn anger into compassion. I handle any person and any situation without anger. Anger blocks my inner-self child abilities to trust, play, and love.

This picture is a symbol of anger. The Gladiator looks symbolically to humanity for thumbs up compassion or thumbs down anger to determine the fate of his downtrodden. The Gladiator transcends when ignoring the advice of the crowd and the

Emperor. He must do the honest courageous work to ignore external influences and own compassion to set this person free! This was taken at the Phoenix Arizona Art Museum.

A mother holding a womb-healed child is the symbol of compassion.

Everyone is born in the 3 = AUM compassion-based transcending light vibrations. Every woman having birthed a baby owns compassion. Every child born owns this same compassion.

I look at my inner-self team and see how I handle anger in any situation. I write this in my diary. When I hold on to anger my life never goes my way.

When I returned to land from my skydiving I remember anger at myself for owning fear in my time before the jump. I was angry with my constant inner-self chatter. Will I live? Will I die? Will the plane crash? Have I accomplished all of my life goals? Am I ready to die? These fear type questions and my constant inner-self chatter took me away from fully enjoying the wonderful airplane ride up and the beautiful day it was.

What job do I do? What relationships do I pick? Where do I go on my transcending light quest? What was the point of fearing? Does my fear give me anything?

Once out of the plane all my fearing and constant inner-self chatter vanished. I was floating through the stillness of space enshrouded by the love of our transcending light vibrations. I owned complete inner-self love for myself.

I never needed to jump out of an airplane and risk my life to own this amazing energy of love. All I needed where sessions with energy healers to let this glorious love shine in. All I needed to do are learn how to meditate and let the love of our divine into my third-eye, heart, body, and soul.

I did not yet fully breathe in the definition of the word transcending until much later on my quest. Anger and fear feed off each other. When I hold anger I also hold fear. There is a reason why a dog or other animal is more likely to attack when sensing fear. They know fear and anger are one and dislike low vibrations.

$$\text{Fear} = \text{Anger} = \text{Conflict} = \text{Illness} = \text{War}$$

TIP Δ - I wait before I act on anything causing anger.
TIP Δ - I handle everything without letting my anger escalate.
TIP Δ - I stop exaggerated fight or flight when I own anger.

Anger is the root of instability and all things terrible. I felt anger when my voice now heard was ignored. Anger caused me to view Pangaea with exaggerated fear, despair, and fight or flight.

TIP Δ - Anger is a sign that old wounds affect me in my now.

TIP Δ - Anger occurred when my set self-discipline is violated.

TIP Δ - Anger occurred when I was not able to own my needs.

My transcending light quest takes me to Phoenix Arizona. My quest takes me on a path through the beautiful Sonora Desert!

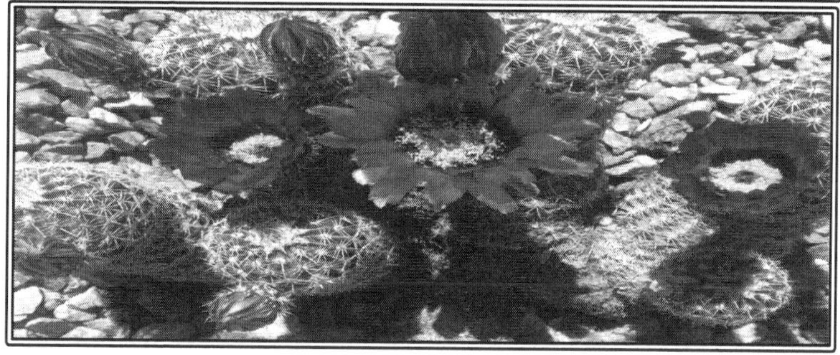

My overwhelming inner-self chatter drove me to keep my cycle of self-pity. I replayed old wounds my parents inflicted on me. I owned the same inner-self critical parenting which kept me from owning my now living. My parent Daniel continued to attack my inner-self child Danny as my parents did many years ago.

In my early twenties I had a beautiful loving relationship with a lady who I went out with. We were getting along fabulously until one day she called me baby and Danny boy. My faced turned red with shame and anger. I yelled at her for having what I thought was criticizing my inner-self child as my parents had.

She was trying to be affectionate, loving, and nurturing by calling out my inner-self child baby Danny boy. This argument caused a loving relationship to fall apart.

TIP Δ - I update my daily diary with the following questions.

Am I closer or further away from anger today?
Am I closer or further away from compassion today?

Anger kept me from healing old wounds. My well-being status was hidden because anger overwhelmed all other moods. I was a zombie going through the motions of living. I saw Pangaea through looking glass despair. Where do my anger moods belong?

They originated from my constant negative inner-self chatter and constant fearing. I desperately needed for my inner-self team to change and go back to my safe, stable, and loving womb-healed days.

Owning anger has me own a false sense of myself – an illusion. Anger has me unable to fill my soul up with our transcending light vibrations "desperately" trying to heal and unconditionally love me.

Anger was all consuming sucking me into a void of despair. I put up a nice guy façade while anger and fear broiled deep down.

TIP Δ – Acknowledging my inner-self love are some tools I use to pull out of anger and burn off old wounds of anger, fear, and illness.

If I have one bad day I can blame my parents upbringing on that, if there is one bad week I can blame my ancestry, if having a bad month I can blame my negative relationships, if it is a bad year I can blame transcending light vibrations. Blame, blame, and more blame. I can play the blame game yet I am always the loser.

This is a vicious circle / every moment of every day I am looking for something to go wrong so it reinforces my old wounds. I become aware of my sad eight hundred pound gorilla of anger. I learned to take this anger and make it into a huggable toy. I start looking around to see the three beams of light at 33 South Third Street in Denver Colorado. I see our 3 compassion-based transcending light vibrations love inside these 3 beams of light!

How did I break this vicious circle?

TIP Δ – I regain loving umbilical cord attachments to transcending light vibrations, inner-self love, and compassion.

My inner-self chatter was feeding my anger to keep pilling up more on top of itself. Years and years go by with piles of new anger on top of old. Anger kept me holding onto the negative vibrating moods of shame, judgment, fear, blame, and despair. I held onto negative low vibrating relationships, events, and environments. It took transcending light quest awareness to heal old wounds.

TIP Δ - I release my anger so I own the positive vibrations of compassion, love, self-esteem, courage, happiness, and success.

TIP Δ - I am what I eat and think. Holding onto anger continuously attracts angry people into my life. Holding onto compassion attracts compassionate people into my life

As I travelled across the country I was publishing new versions of my diary and sending them to people for reviews. I corresponded with friends, talk shows, and families about how to "complete" this diary. Everyone was excited to read about all the topics my quest shone a light upon. When I wrote from anger I was so fogged up my writings did not heal and help others the way I knew they could.

TIP Δ - My anger blocked me from writing from my heart. I needed to learn how to connect my mind to my heart and body so they work in synchronicity. I can then write and speak life truths.

TIP Δ - Sometimes it seems everyone is for himself or herself. Compassion might seem hard to find. I look around and find the compassion of humanity.

The 3 = 🕉 symbol heals humanity in 201 🕉 and beyond!

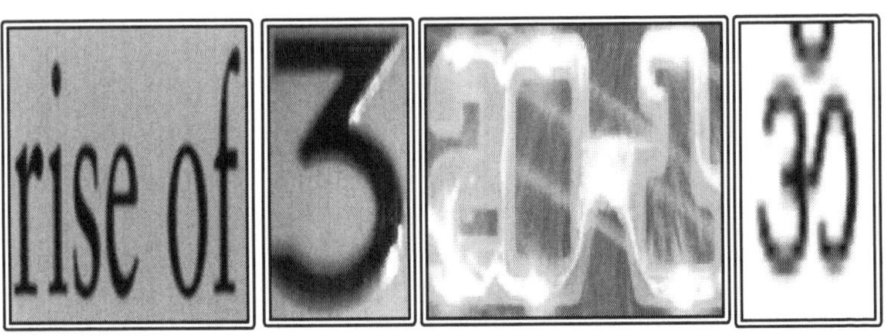

TIP Δ – At the moment of anger, I own compassion.
TIP Δ – I can take part in things I dislike without owning anger.

I own a compassion-based journey.

The word danger has the word anger in it. Acting on anger can be dangerous. At times it might seem humanity lacks compassion. I discovered the truth on my transcending light quest. Hundreds of "strangers" gave me compassion and they did not have to.

TIP Δ – Strangers gave me water, food, and shelter on the trails.
TIP Δ – Strangers warned me of a car about to run me over.
TIP Δ – Strangers kept me from owning an early morgue toe tag.

The longer I hold on to anger the more it wounds me. I rid the wounds of anger to heal my inner-self team. I observe my well-being every day and write it in my diary. I focus on getting beyond anger so my human compassion shines.

My walks through trails and parks delete my anger.
I hiked past many Appalachian Trail markers to heal.

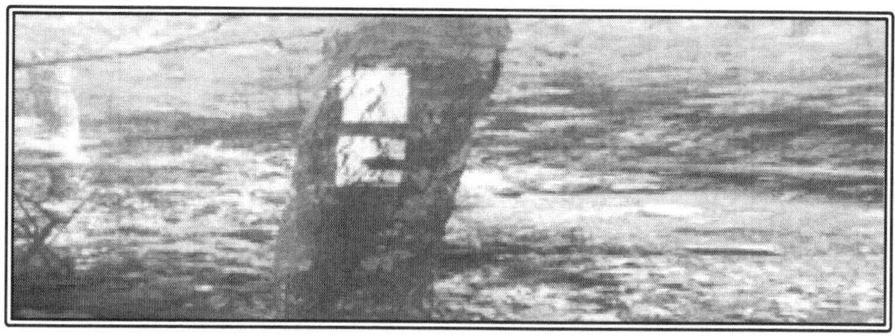

MHC is helping everyone own compassion.

I almost became an Eagle Boy Scout at age fifteen. This is the highest rank in scouting. The only remaining thing for me to do was pick up trash on the interstate. I wanted to do this yet the troop leadership fell apart. There was no stability-healing hero to guide me. I always wished my Mother could pin an eagle badge on my uniform.

TIP Δ – Taking out the trash of others is a symbol of compassion.

TIP Δ – Charities are devoted to cleaning up messes of others.

TIP Δ - The eagle is a symbol of compassionate leadership.

TIP Δ - The eagle owns healing and equal human civil rights for all.

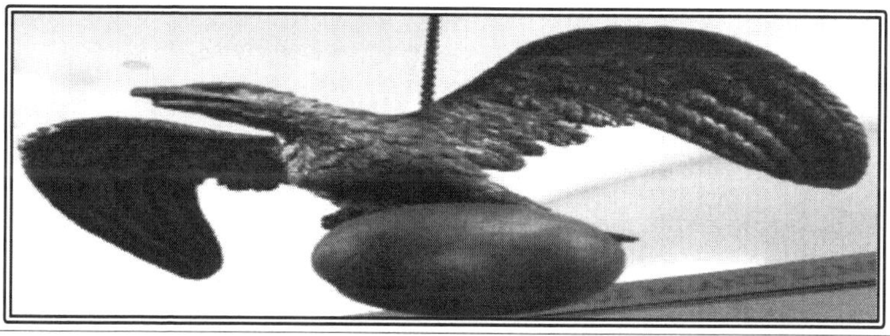

I am open to compassion-based listening and well-being availability.

I ask compassion-based questions to encourage others to explain important things. Compassion owns perfect peace for Pangaea.

TIP Δ - I own well-being availability.

These questions help me determine the compassion of others.

TIP Δ - Is the person I am with genuinely interested in me?
TIP Δ - Can this person demonstrate well-being availability?
TIP Δ - Is this person able to own compassion-based listening?
TIP Δ - Are they concerned with healing themselves and others?
TIP Δ – Do they own stability on a daily basis?

These answers help me decide to cuts or attach cord relationships.

A Mother holding her baby is my reminder that compassion is alive and well within our humanity.

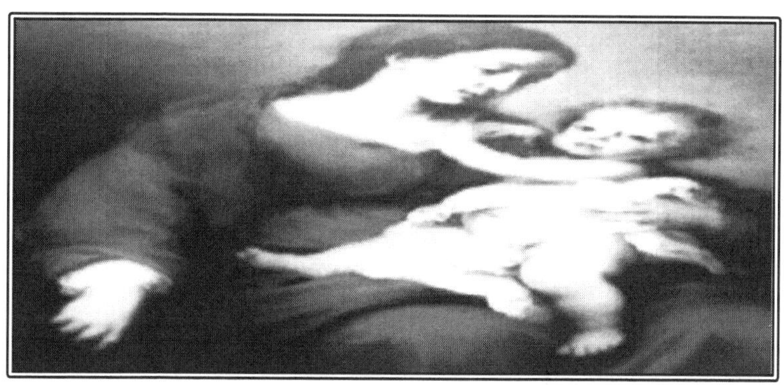

This is a picture of my shadow aura in a moving sign in Atlanta, Georgia. I moved away from this city of my old wounds.

When it is raining it rains on all of us. When it is sunshine it is shining on all of us. Transcending light vibrations does not make choices. The one spirit lives in all. We pray for everyone. We meditate for everyone. Peace to all, life to all, and love to all.

My life had left me being an actor in my own life. I own honest courageous work to shatter this. Sometimes life seems to be a bunch of randomly taped together events. When I look around I find compassion everywhere. The old friends giving gentle hugs for each other, the Mother kissing their baby as they go off to a first day of school, and the stranger who helps a sensory stability hero get their wheel chair onto the bus. The anonymous donor who gives millions to help homeless veterans have a safe and stable home of their own.

Every day I write in my diary the new compassions I see and hear. I become a hero healer advocate and learn as much as I can.

TIP Δ - I learned to stop living in the questions so I could start existing in the answers.

The high vibrating energy coming in from our age of Aquarius is reconstructing us at the gneetic levels. We are all healing from the inside out. The Angels and Divine Feminine energy is enshrouding each of us with the full forces of healing.

Are you ready for quick changes? Are you ready to move quickly? MHC will show you how to make quick changes for rapid growth. I teach how to act quickly and survive in unfavorable and uncomfortable conditions. I demonstrate keen eyesight along with expanding awareness in many transcending light directions. Don't be scared – MHC is right here by your side.

This picture is the symbol of My Human Compassion having a compassion-based ear out to hear humanities stories of suffering, compassion, and overcoming.

Each of the over 7.2 billion in humanity will become a billionaire. The MHC evolutionary movement creates evenly distributed economic, political, and humanitarian realities. We learn how to transcend smoothly into the new Age of Aquarius.

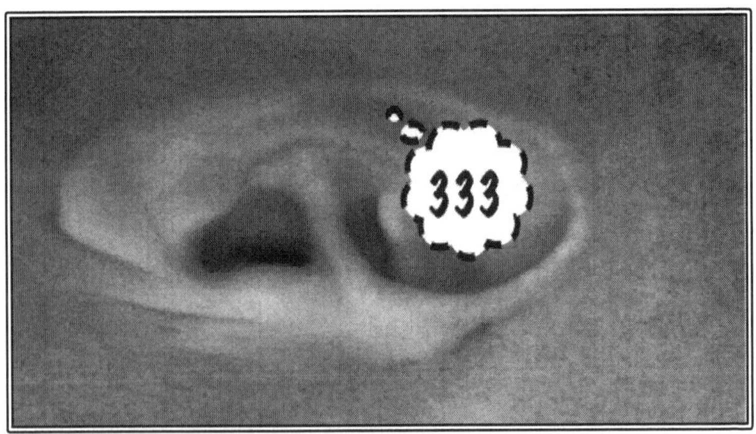

Anyone can hit rock bottom. At one time I did not believe in rock bottom ownership. I was about to learn all about it.

Stability-Healing Questions

How does MHC turn anger to compassion?

Owning anger is a personal choice, how does this help heal MHC?

What positives does anger block from MHC?

How can MHC own needs?

What are the MHC signs of anger?

What anger provoking things does MHC needs to be aware of?

How does MHC prove that humanity is mostly compassionate?

How does MHC observing inner-self well-being stop anger?

How cans MHC own perfect peace?

What does the transcending light quest teach MHC about humanity?

Why would strangers save MHC from an early morgue toe tag?

Why is a Mother and a baby the symbol of compassion?

What does the symbol of the eagle teach MHC?

How can compassion-based testing help heal MHC?

Chapter 12 Rock Bottom Ownership

Rock Bottom Dan
Will It Be?
All Humanity Healed?
This One Life
However Self-Broken
How To Heal?
What Can I Do?
Forgiveness Healing Now
So I Can
Help Heal Others
Teaching My Values
Set Self-Discipline
Inner-Influenced Actions
Safety, acceptance, and stability
Inner-Self Love
Compassion-Based Healing
I Reach New
Rock Bottom Ownership
To Rise Again
Life Is Transcending

TIP Δ - It is a great honor for me to truly own what someone says.

TIP Δ - It is my great honor to give my human compassion.

Exaggerated well-being signs of my father were that he was unable to sleep, his conversations rambled, and he took impulsive actions without thinking through their results. He ignored daily responsibilities. He drank alcohol to numb his pain of old wounds. He had a false fear that everyone and everything was out to hurt him. Abusive Father Forgiven often refused stability medication.

Abusive Father Forgiven had cruel tendencies yet they would have owned calming had he taken stability medication. On a snowy, icy night during the 1970s Abusive Father Forgiven owned crisis. Angry Mother Forgiven had to get his sedatives fast!

The snowy ice-filled streets had steep hills. This area proved dangerous even in clear weather. It was the 1970s and cars in those days did not have the snow tires of today. This New York picture is a symbol of those dangerous driving conditions.

TIP Δ – My Mother avoided divorce thinking she would be broke.

This was the 1970s where women suffered along in marriage without owning divorce. In the past, the main role of a wife was to remain at home and take care of the house. If a divorce occurred, a wife could be left homeless. In those days, there were fewer shelters to help mothers own safety from domestic abuse.

TIP Δ – It took years for my Mother to own courage for divorce.
TIP Δ – Permanent cutting of long-term umbilical cords is not easy.

If a father does abuse, a Mother abuses, or a partner abuses in any of these scenarios, the umbilical cord must be cut. Father, Mother, and or Parents paying their child money for having their needs met. Partner paying money for another partner to own needs.

TIP Δ – No amount of money gives anyone a right to abuse.

My parent's self-destructive marriage went on far longer than it should have because of the money my father paid my mother. My Human Compassion is in a 3-road race to heal humanity.

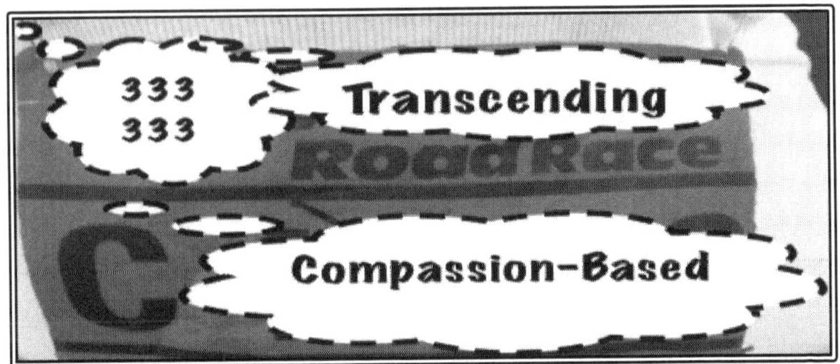

My stability-healing hero responsibilities define me. I am defined by how I observe and stabilize my well-being. I am defined by how I own my needs and help others. During my transcending light quest I stumbled through dangerous situations. I could have been another statistic.

A mid-life male found with no money or identification. A drifter unable to own anywhere called home. A person who never owned they're true-life-purpose. The cause of death was an inability to own needs. Dan Doe slipped off of a cliff in the Appalachian Trail. Dan Doe died in the wilderness from disease infested food and water. A car killed Dan Doe while walking through a red light. Dan Doe died in a homeless shelter. My transcending light quest "hit" me with looking glass reality.

This hit potential is never far away from anyone. Having faced my reality hit I realized how fortunate I am to awaken up and own stability-healing hero support.

TIP Δ – Anyone can hit rock bottom ownership and rise up.

This picture symbolizes my daily rock bottom ownership. I am at the bottom of a rock at Garden of the Gods in Colorado. This is the base of Pikes Peak Mountain Colorado.

I cut my umbilical cord with Hyper-Love Forgiven. This hurled my well-being into crisis. All of my hard earned money faded away.

I compassion-based listen to the inspiration, passion, and honest courageous work many heroes must own to overcome any illness. I reach out to my stability-healing heroes and trusted healers.

Researching all medical options is a great thing.

I learned to say, "I need help" when owning crisis. I am not afraid to share my honest well-being with others. I set self-discipline to own an inner-self protected. The ceremony of Intervention saved my brother – Beyond Rock Bottom - from owning an early death. I took this skull and cross bones painted on a rock while hiking in the Appalachian Trails.

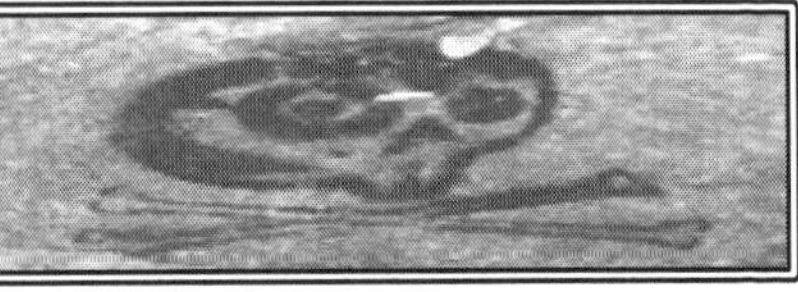

Intervention is when a family faces another person to get them help. After intervention the person must choose treatment or not. There are treatment centers open twenty-four hours a day. Intervention is an emergency ceremony that can save lives.

Beyond Rock Bottom views beautiful scenery for the first time.
This is near the Grand Canyon at Horse Shoe Bend in Page Arizona.

Instability and unhealthy eating left me with an inner-self void. This was taken near the top of Camel Back Mountain in Phoenix Arizona.

If things appear looking glass chaotic this is temporary. There is another stable day to be lived. Never-give-up! This is how healing music gets tattooed on my inner-self team. This picture is at the Great Sand Dunes National Park Colorado.

TIP Δ - Positive support groups teach us how to own our needs.

TIP Δ – Well-being availability supports my 🕉 safety.

Intervention gave my brother Beyond Rock Bottom a sober journey.

TIP Δ - This is the template letter getting Beyond Rock Bottom into treatment. This template letter saves lives.

Dear ___________,

I am here because I love you and I need to help you. I am not here to hurt you or betray you. I realize you are an adult and you make your own actions however your family is demanding you own a new direction in your future. I have owned worry about you for many years. I have not known how to tell you this.

Today, our family decided to get together in sharing our concerns with you. I have always loved you and I will always love you. I need the best for you. I have always looked up at you and seen you as a <insert family role> for many years.

I have seen you owning <insert addiction, self-abuse, brain instability, etc.> I own <insert embarrassed, angry, sad, hurt, etc.> to be around you when you are doing <insert negative action(s), addiction, instability, self-abuse, etc.>.

The words I am about to tell you are difficult because I do not want them to be misunderstood. I tell you these words while making sure you know our transcending light vibrations own zero shame, zero guilt, zero blame, and zero judgments.

I own these words to help you own a new direction and to own positive changes. I have owned fear to tell you over the years how <insert angry, embarrassed, sad, hurt, etc.> I am because you might be angry with me. I am concerned about the <insert action(s) e.g. substance abuse, self-abuse, instability, etc.> you have owned for <insert years>. I do what I can do to help heal you.

I cannot make you do anything. Only you can change for your inner-self team. You are an adult. I do not want you to die or harm an innocent family. I need you to live! With your current actions of <insert self-abuse, addiction, instability, etc.> you will die from <insert e.g. affects on your body, kill an innocent family with drunk driving, prison, homelessness, bankruptcy, hospitalization, institutionalization, or own an early morgue toe tag>. Never-give-up!

I need to see the day when you will overcome <insert action(s), instability, addiction, etc.> to own the treatments to heal. You gambled with your own life and faced your sufferings alone. Do not be discouraged! I clearly see the road to your freedom built with treatment, therapy, and honest courageous healing work.

I need you to take positive actions and enter a treatment center immediately after this intervention. You will be safe, accepted, and stable at this compassion-based treatment center the family found. This center owns education, medication, and tools you need to stop <insert self-abuse action(s), illness, substance abuse, abuse, etc.>.

I realize you have been there for me during multiple times in my life. This is my chance to be there to save your life. I need you to overcome your <insert action(s) e.g. illness, substance abuse, etc.>. I will benefit and the family benefits when you stop <insert self-abuse action(s), illness, substance abuse, instability, etc.>.

I Love You: _______________ <insert name>

TIP Δ - Intervention released my brother's inner-self team from a prison of negative ancestral routines.

I took this picture at Harpers Ferry West Virginia in a prison armory John Brown held for one day back in 1859. John and his supporters took this armory as an act against slavery. This action sparked the beginning of the Civil War in 1861, which would abolish slavery and split the state into two separate entities.

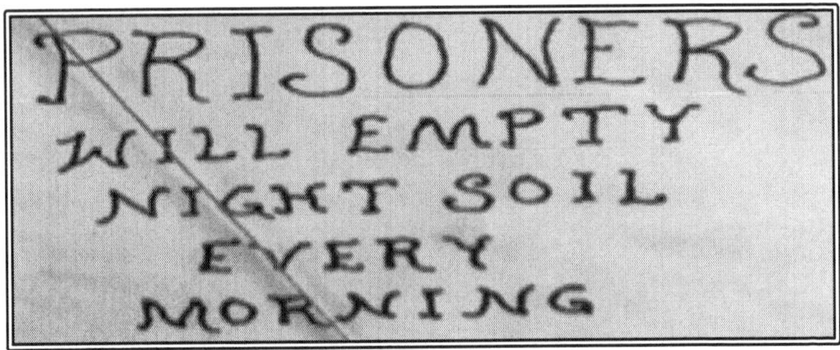

As I transcend my journey, the names inner-self love, inner-self playful, voice now heard, inner-self woman, inner-self man, inner-self forgiven, others-self forgiven, and my human compassion are educated to own safety, acceptance, and stability. This is how I add inner-self protected, voice now validated, compassion-based parent, and inner-self transcending to my inner-self team. These are what help me own a voice now validated.

TIP Δ - I own a voice now heard with child-like trust and no fears.
TIP Δ - I own a voice now heard with child-like trust I will be heard.
TIP Δ - I own a voice now heard with child-like trust to own needs.

As a young adult, an unstable well-being started to challenge me. I learned to say, "I need help" to stability-healing heroes. During adolescence, I gradually separated my inner-self team from my parents and I began parenting myself. My compassion-based parent works to own my needs. The next years show my transcending from Danny to Dan.

My inner-self team changed from teenager to adult. These are difficult times. I wish I had lived by the inner-stability pyramid rules. These guidelines could have spared me from suffering.

My times of exaggerated joy and exaggerated despair ran together as one. Ideas of owning life as being only negative or positive got exaggerated. In despair I focused on myself. During joy I focused on everyone but me. I needed to own the present.

There is no time like the present!

As a kid, I watched the television program *Bionic Woman*. She had her ear replaced with a defective bionic ear. It was supposed to own super hearing however she heard hundreds of conversations all at once. She screamed in agonizing pain. These overwhelming stimuli of senses caused her exaggerated instability. She fell to the ground and owned a shut down reboot.

This was super flawed!

This story echoed within me. It represents a view of life with an exaggerated well-being. The inner-self team can only handle so many stimuli before reaching shut down. My well-being of exaggerated joy and overwhelming despair result in my brain getting overloaded from hearing, touch, taste, sight, and smelling along with happy, sad, and or anger. As part of being enrolled in humanity I juggle many things.

This art depicts beyond rock bottom to rise up from there. This art shows transcending light vibrations that heal us.

The art above is by Shamie Encinas at ShamArt44@yahoo.com. It is an excellent way to show beyond rock bottom. Our transcending reaches bottom yet our transcending light vibrations continuously heal us at this bottom. We are never defeated and humanity will "be prepared" to deal with whatever comes our way.

How do I avoid danger?
Whom must I encounter?
What business must I pursue?
Which commitments do I make?
What education do I need?
What events must I attend?
I learn to overcome this constant inner-self chatter.

This campsite is a symbol of where I met strangers who helped me create this 3-question and 3-answer based diary.

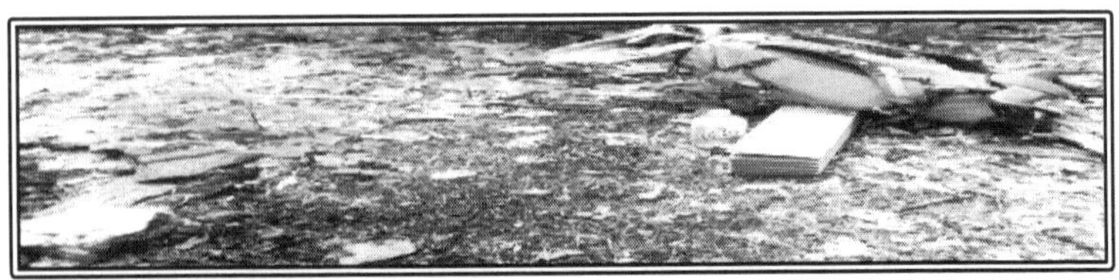

My transcending owned exaggerated sad, happy, anger, fear, joy, hearing, touching, tasting, sight, and smell all at once. On top of this overload I had to deal with daily routines of business, events, hobbies, and attempting to eat nutritious meals.

I salute veteran stability heroes and sensory stability heroes. This diary is a tribute for all veteran stability heroes.

The next chapter explores how all of these types of overloads can cause my inner-self team to go into a shut down reboot. I learn how to overcome a shut down reboot so I can live in the now.

Stability-Healing Questions

What are the great honors for MHC?

What are the exaggerated well-being signs of the Father of MHC?

How does the Father of MHC cover up old wounds?

How does beyond rock bottom help heal MHC?

What are the things that truly define MHC?

Why does the Mother of MHC stay in a relationship far too long?

What was MHC hit with during the transcending light quest?

How can the MHC intervention letter help heal?

How does intervention help heal the brother of MHC?

How does a positive support group help heal MHC?

How is addiction a negative ancestry in the family of MHC?

How does owning zero tolerance for abuse help heal MHC?

What honest courageous work did the Mother of MHC do?

How does MHC own a voice now validated?

Chapter 13 Shut Down Reboot

Exaggerated Joy Dan
Exaggerated Despair Dan
Water Overflows Everywhere!
Cappuccino Like Froth
Flowing Forward Backwards
Overpowering Furious Pace
Transcending Golden Healed
Consuming Stones Twigs
Downside Upside Now!
Well-Being Availability
Hail Once Known
All Mighty Froth
Is No More
Shut Down Reboot?
What Gathers Strength?
To Form Again
As I Look
South East West
North Even More
Rivers Again Gaining
Strength As Before
Fear And Fearlessness
All Swirling Together
Senses Stability Tools
Stability Owned Now!

A certainty on my unique transcending journey is humanity facing constant continual change. Owning exaggerations I thought anything is possible.

TIP Δ – My human civil rights give me freedom of thoughts.

TIP Δ – I am not accountable for what my thoughts are.

TIP Δ – I am responsible for my actions and their results.

Owning unstable thoughts overwhelm my inner-self team. My exaggerated well-being shut me down.

Sights?   Joy? Fear? Anger? Happy? Sad? Fear? Joy? Fear?
Sounds? Joy? Fear? Anger? Happy? Sad? Fear? Joy? Fear?
Touch?   Joy? Fear? Anger? Happy? Sad? Fear? Joy? Fear?
Moods? Joy? Fear? Anger? Happy? Sad? Fear? Joy? Fear?
Smells? Joy? Fear? Anger? Happy? Sad? Fear? Joy? Fear?
Tastes? Joy? Fear? Anger? Happy? Sad? Fear? Joy? Fear?

My exaggerated well-being results in inner-self team closure. This is a Marta train closure sign in Atlanta, Georgia.

Exaggerations sent my inner-self team into spacey instability. This is a space suit at the science center in Denver Colorado.

During my Dan years, I struggled with daily well-being statuses ranging from negative to positive and back to positive.

Exaggerations kept me from finishing simple tasks. Others easily took advantage of me when I owned instability.

Passion is important for living; humanity must have humans who are passionate leaders to help others find their way. There is a fine line between allowing passion and taking medication numbing a person into a zombie. This is a medical treatment dilemma. How much instability should one own? How much passion and moods should one own?

TIP Δ – Healers cannot over-medicate.

TIP Δ – Healers cannot under-medicate.

It is my non-clinical view seven hours of sleep is mandatory for owning stability. With an exaggerated well-being and lacking sleep I need to share the huge beauty and intense passions of Pangaea. I took this inside the New York City Museum Of Art. I viewed an exaggerated enormously beautiful life.

An exaggerated well-being overwhelmed me!

TIP Δ – Humanity needs people to own crying, laughing, and joy.

I did not yet know a way to enter and monitor my inner-self team.

TIP Δ – Exaggerated despair owns looking glass paralyzed living.
TIP Δ – Exaggerated joy owns looking glass paralyzed living.

I could do anything. Underneath my super hero disguise deep down connecting with my soul I owned despair. Meditation to this statue and transcending light vibrations restores my harmony. I took the picture of an Asian statue at the Phoenix, Arizona Art Museum.

TIP Δ – Stable-senses tools fire extinguishes my instability.

TIP Δ – I must be well-being honest with those I trust.
TIP Δ – I get healing from the crystals, quartz, and stones I own.

Topaz	Rose Quartz	Crystal Points	Sapphire	Obsidian
Smokey	Moon Stone	Amethyst	Emerald	Fluorite

   Sight, sound, touch, hear, taste, and moods rush into my well-being at once. My senses are overloaded. When I experienced this overload I had this overwhelming exaggeration of stimuli rushing into my well-being all at once. I experience what I call a "shut down". I had to go home and go to bed. It was transcending light vibrations, sleep, medications, and stability-healing heroes that enabled me to "reboot" and get back to living. I own the tools to prevent myself from owning a shut down reboot.

TIP Δ – A thought comes so I own the time to act on it or ignore it.
TIP Δ – If the thought goes against my core values I ignore it.
TIP Δ – I get support before making major life decisions.

Overwhelming visual, noise, or sight environments increase the chances of shut down reboot and unnecessary trips to a healer. Sensory stability heroes must be careful about places they visit. Parents can be careful of places they put their children in.

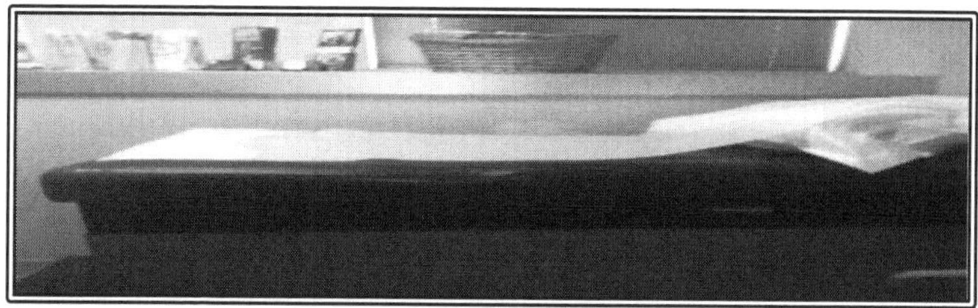

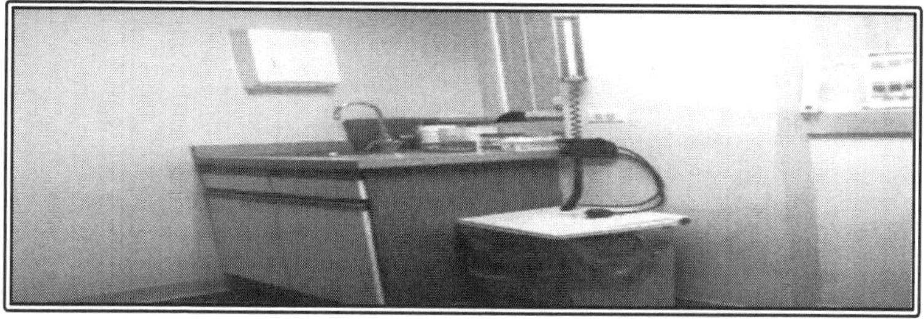

An exaggerated well-being might "seem" to be lasting forever. It is not forever! This is simply a day and it will pass. A day gets stable when I own stable-senses tools and stability-healing hero support. A brand new healed day is around the corner. I create inner-self team alliance with stability-healing heroes.

During my times of exaggerated joy I had moments where I thought I was here to save humanity. I came to realize it is not just me who can save all of us. It takes the over seven billion of humanity working together to bring healing to us all.

The teachings of humanity coming to an end "end of days" are all false. This type of popular thinking is poisonous to humanity.

I met a wonderful person on my travels who is homeless. He used to work as an administrator in creating new homeless shelters. He used to help run programs to house and feed our homeless. It turns out that he recently adopted the view that humanity is in a time of end of days. Because he adopted this type of thinking he stopped doing all the hard work he used to do in helping others. He is resolved to spend his time waiting for end of days that will not happen. I told him that it is not end of days. This is a time of healing. People have been predicting the end of world since the beginning of humanity. End of day predictions are a poison for the positive transcending of humanity.

When it is time for anyone to own an after-life and fold back into our transcending light vibrations we restart womb-healed regardless of whether we owned healed or not. Transcending light vibrations owns equal love for every member of humanity. Writers of any of the types of fearing texts did not own their needs. They created text based on brain instability and a need to control others. The meaning of life question has many answers.

TIP Δ - Humanity heals when leaders own first nation-healing.

TIP Δ - Life owns transcending light vibrations.

TIP Δ - Life owns compassion and inner-self love.

TIP Δ – Life owns equal inner-self woman and inner-self man.

I worship my inner-self love using my senses of taste, hearing, seeing, smelling, touching, a stable well-being, and transcending.

My inner-self team focuses on how to own stability.

I worship life is transcending first nation-healing including the sun, trees, plants, water, ocean, earth, mountains, senses, moods, transcending light vibrations, and humanity.

Two babies are born. One set of parents is first-nation healing and the other couple is atheist. The hospital accidently swaps the babies to the wrong set of parents. A baby supposed to be first-nation healing is raised atheist and a baby supposed to be atheist is raised first-nation healing. These babies are tested on their unique journey with their unique diary questions and answers. The results of questioning and answering determine the baby's transcending.

One night in college I decided to rewrite the encyclopedia. I started with the letter A. I was up all night working on this. I truly believed I was on to a wonderful break through revolutionizing Pangaea. My unique passionate version would improve the writings in all the ways it lacked. My encyclopedia rewrite owned an understanding it lacked. My ideas were creatively flowing through me as I rewrote A. In one night, I wrote over thirty pages for this section. Then I got to the word alligator. I reached a wall of exhaustion and I could not write any more. I was trying to write *Looking Glass Shattered* but I lacked the life experiences to complete it. Writing this diary has been my greatest gift to humanity and myself.

This is a picture of a bus I boarded in Aurora Colorado. I welcome aboard my new journey to transcending.

Looking glass shattered owns my transcending.

Owning instability caused me unnecessary life sufferings. During my transcending light quest, I spent all of my retirement and savings I accumulated over twenty years. It was over $33,333 and a lot of was given to Hyper-Love Forgiven without expecting anything in return. My instability allowed others to drive through me. This is a drive through I came across in Atlanta, Georgia

TIP Δ - Next time I fall in love I own unconditional love disciplined.

I never thought when I was buying Hyper-Love Forgiven five hundred dollar boots, four hundred dollar blouses, a five thousand dollar painting, and a thousand dollar ring it would be my Mother who would pay for those items. She helped bail me out of debt and I bailed myself out by getting back to work. My Mother won't always be around to bail me out. I have to always own prepared so I never again risk well-being bankruptcy. I can do it all myself.

We can create a place where first nation-healing is taught. All ethnicities and sexual orientation are welcome. We do inner-self prayer/meditation to heal humanity and Pangaea. We worship inner-self love and transcending light vibrations. We teach the positive core values of our stability-healing heroes.

I was riding the light rail in Phoenix Arizona and I saw a 3333 address. I had to get off and take a picture. I was amazed when I discovered that this building is the Veterans Administration!

A Mandala is from a Sanskrit word-meaning circle. It is a symbol of the circle of life. It reminds me of my relationship to the 3 of the earth, sun, and moon and a 3 of friends, family, and community. It is our beautiful picture of our continuously expanding universe at any given snapshot in time. I have seen many first-nation cultures creating a Mandala pattern in their own unique way.

I took this picture at the Denver art museum of a movie called "The Wheel Of Healing" about the early 1990s when there was a lot of youth violence in Denver Colorado. Monks from Tibet came to Denver and created this sand made mandala made of sand. When they were finished they scattered this sand Mandala in a local river while praying for peace. Did the Mandala and prayers for peace truly work? Well the city is a much more peaceful place today. Let the wheels of healing roll to every city and countryside.

I have been going back and forth between the wilderness and cities. This raised interesting societal questions and answers concerning external influences, fearing, transcending, survival, needs, laws, human civil rights, tribes, heroes, fantasy, home, homelessness, attachments, communal living, courage, core values, compassion, anger, stability, ancestry, first nation, history, culture, equality, justice, liberty, environmentalism, and freedom.

TIP Δ - Healing Pangaea burdens transcends compassion.

The inner-stability pyramid is a tool for observing and stabilizing my well-being. I own this tool and my diaries to share liberty, equality, justice, freedom, and compassion. These are inserted into my time capsule for my descendants to enjoy.

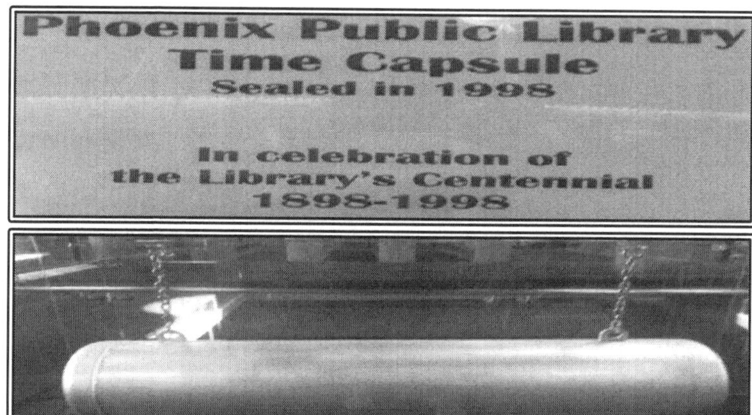

I take caution about people and situations I walk into. This was taken at the YMCA I stayed at in Phoenix, Arizona. This elevator was being repaired and I am glad I saw the caution tape and did not walk into it!

The food pyramid teaches foods to eat for owning stability. The inner-stability pyramid teaches how to own well-being stability. I observe my well-being every day so I may own stability. These prevent entry into the inner-stability pyramid.

Looking Glass Shattered

My Human Compassion validates all illnesses and sufferings.
Compassion owns my life shadow to transcend bolder and deeper!

Stability-Healing Questions

How does MHC owning the freedom of thoughts heal?

How does owning responsibility for actions help heal MHC?

What is shut down reboot and how does it affect MHC?

Why does MHC believe fearing hurts humanity?

How can MHC stop owning a shut down reboot?

Why does MHC believe exaggerated joy and despair is forever?

How did external influences prevent MHC from healing?

What stimuli flooded MHC all at once?

How can transcending light vibrations heal MHC?

What tools prevent MHC from owning a shut down reboot?

How does well-being honesty heal MHC?

What does MHC write in the diary about his experiences?

How does the Mandala help heal MHC?

How can MHC own a bolder deeper life?

Chapter 14 Inner-Stability Pyramid

Fight Or Flight?
Brain Stabilized Dan
It's My Responsibility!
Celebrating Living Now
Compassioned-Based Transcending
Unique Transcending Journey
Inner-Self Healed!
All Pangaea Tribes
Inner-Self Aware!
Guiding My Journey
Inner-Self Love
Child-Adult-Parent
Joy Despair Overcoming
Replaced Forever Stable
Life Is Transcending
Looking Glass Shattered!
I Am Owning
Well-Being Availability
Compassion-Based Listening
Humanity Compassioned Together!

My sad, fear, anger, needs, and thankful statements help me heal.

TIP Δ – Sad.

I am sad I might be unable to move beyond old wounds.
I am sad I am unable to get the loving relations I deserve.
I am sad that no one needs me and I haven't found a partner.

TIP Δ – Fear.

I fear that I cannot find stability-healing heroes.
I fear that I am unable to own my needs or help others own theirs.
I fear I am unable to own safety, acceptance, and stability.
I fear that I cannot regain my child-like trust of love.

TIP Δ – Anger.

I am angry past partners lacked compassion.
I am angry that I allowed external influences to control me.
I am angry that I did not own inner-influenced actions.

TIP Δ – Needs.

I must own unconditional love disciplined.
I must be in stability-healing hero relationships.
I must forgive all of my former partners.
I must regain my child-like trust of others.

TIP Δ – Inner-Self Forgiven rids fear and anger to own now.
TIP Δ – Others-Self Forgiven rids fear and anger to own now.

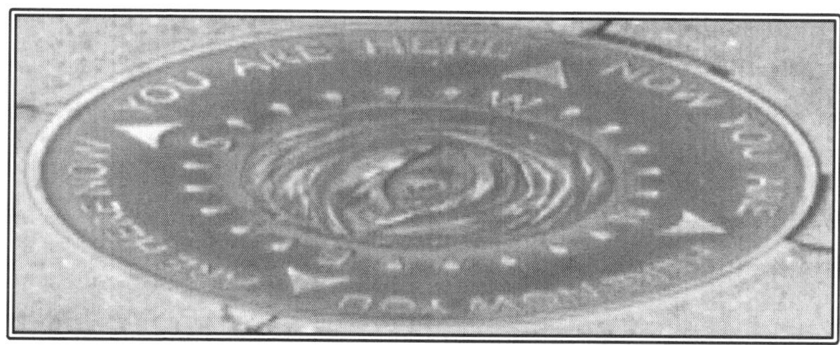

Dolphins are a symbol of child-like trust to own new love. This was taken in Midtown Atlanta Georgia near a coffee shop where I worked on this diary.

TIP Δ – I am thankful my fear, sadness, anger, and love are stable.
TIP Δ – I am thankful for the love I own and the love I will find.
TIP Δ – I am thankful of tools stabilizing my well-being.
TIP Δ – I am thankful for stability-healing heroes.

I acted on fear when there was no fear. I acted on joy when there was no joy. I had intense needs to cry when there was nothing to cry about. I used defensive flight or flight when I did not need to. I saw danger when there was no danger. I saw Pangaea through an exaggerated fight or flight lens. An exaggerated well-being warns me.

When I was unstable my inner-self voice now heard had many messages to say yet they were all blurry, upside down, and I did not know how to combine them to say, "I need help" for stability-healing hero support.

I learned to not get trapped in exaggerations. I stay alive! This photo was taken at Tombstone Arizona.

I own my inner-self team 3 = ॐ to unlock my old wounds and own stability. I took this picture on the Maryland side of the bridge of Harpers Ferry West Virginia. West Virginia is on one side of the bridge and Maryland is on the other.

I own Inner-Stability Pyramid to push out of any emergency.

TIP Δ - I am the only one inside my head.

TIP Δ - My well-being is based on my thoughts.

TIP Δ - I own complete control of my inner-self team.

TIP Δ - I decide if my actions are positive or negative.

TIP Δ - I write daily questions and answers in my diary.

TIP Δ - I take these writings to trusted healers and support.

TIP Δ - The healer is always in - I am my healer of healers.

This is my evolutionary diary that heals humanity.

TIP Δ – I heal with transcending light vibrations.
TIP Δ – I own stable-senses tools and positive actions.
TIP Δ – I use patience to own my appropriate actions.
TIP Δ – My feet walk my journey owning patience.

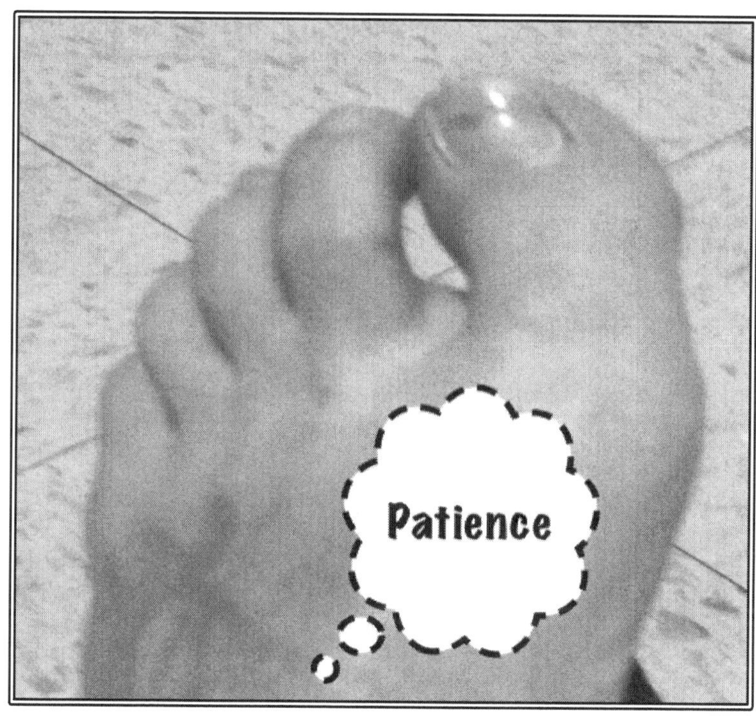

TIP Δ - I resolve arguments and help others own their needs.
TIP Δ - I avoid fight or flight.
TIP Δ - These are diary questions for my inner-stability pyramid.

Why do I own an exaggerated well-being at this moment?
What is the root source as to why I own this particular mood?
Am I sleepy, hungry, in pain, or in need of affection?
Am I in love, lonely, sad, angry, or fearful?
What are my transcending needs for my present and future?

How can I replace anger with compassion?

The food pyramid teaches foods to eat for owning stability. The inner-stability pyramid teaches how to own a stable well-being. I observe my well-being so I may own stability. I cannot enter the inner-stability pyramid if any of the following are true.

I do not own my	stable-senses tools.
I do not own my	well-being honesty.
I own moods	based on anger or rage.
I own moods	of exaggerated fight or flight.
I own an	exaggerated well-being.
I own either	self-abuse or abuse.

TIP Δ - Every day owns my new well-being changes.

TIP Δ - I own my life inside the pyramid or outside of it.

My inner-stability pyramid owns a well-being status in full view. This pyramid is made up of five different layers. The first layers are my highest priority.

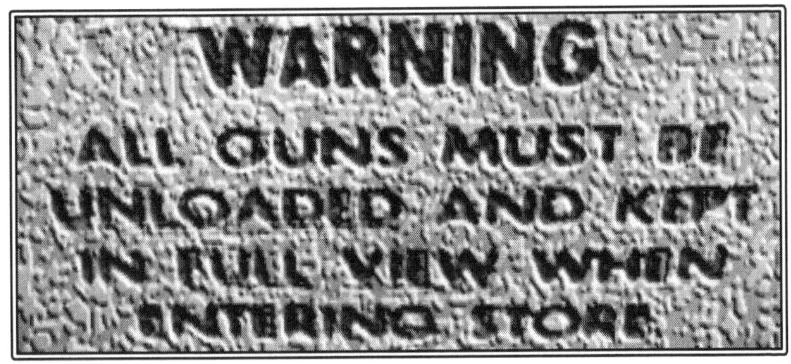

In the "first pyramid layer" I am aware of what I need to own my needs and stability. I am honest to others and myself about my current well-being. I own safety, acceptance, and stability.

My "second pyramid layer" owns well-being availability and compassion-based listening. The "third pyramid layer" replaces low vibrating fear, sadness, or anger with high vibrating courage, happiness, love, forgiveness, thankfulness, and compassion. The "fourth pyramid layer" is my awareness of my inner-self transcending status. The "fifth pyramid layer" is when I own my human civil rights needs and own the needs of others through "mutual compassionate-compromise". My inner-self pyramid owns safety!

Happy, sad, or fearful, I face these well-being changes every day. Suddenly anger emerges. Anger kicks me out of the pyramid.

Anger is the root of all exaggerated fight or flight.
Anger is the root of violence, abuse, self-abuse, and war.

Anger dominates over all other well-being statuses. When I know where my anger comes from, I can stabilize my well-being.

Anger has me own instability.
Anger prevents me from being alive-owning-now.
Anger prevents me from owning an inner-self playful child.
Anger to compassion brings these stabilizing messages to reality.

Shall I tread lightly?
Shall I own permanent everlasting footprints?

Will You Leave No Trace?

I leave a trace through MHC writings, speeches, and charity. Set self-discipline may be elusive when I am only focused on meeting the needs of others.

I Was Taking Care Of Everyone But Me.

I used to be dominated by an eight-hundred pound gorilla of old wounds. A gorilla represents my Abusive Father Forgiven, 911 fears, and old wounds. This gorilla continued to clutch the twin towers long since 911. It continued to push me into a life of despair.

I refuse to continue feeding my old wounded Gorilla with low vibration banannas of anger, fear, sadness, resentment, and blame. When I remove these low vibrations the Gorilla vanishes forever. I eat high vibration bananas of love, peace, joy, hapiness, and success.

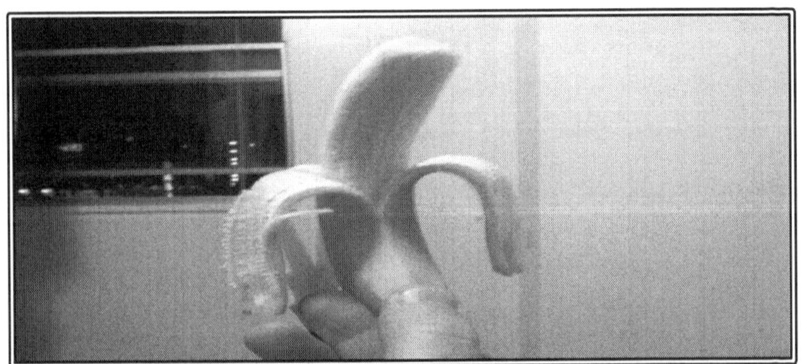

119-fearlessness sets the date back to a time before 911. I was at the Piedmont Marta stop in Atlanta, Georgia and a sign had the date of February 10, 2000 and this was taken in July of 2012.

At time of success or accomplishments; irrational fears would surface taking away my ability to own success. I own my inner-self 119-fearlessness to reverse fears.

I am responsible for learning how to heal my inner-self team.
I am responsible to stabilize my well-being and own my needs.
I am responsible to be honest with my healers.
I am responsible for healing myself so I can heal others.

I update my diary.

How is my diet and do I need to eat?
Do I need to go to bed and own sleep?
Do I need to spend time in nature, hiking, or in the park?
Do I need inner-self meditation and or inner-self prayer?
Must I attach to this umbilical cord or cut this one?
How do I own a budget to live within my means?
How do I define my inner-self home?
How am I well-being available?
How am I compassion-based listening?
I reverse my dead-end 911 fears to 119-fearlessness.

I own first nation-healing so healing politics will begin. This is a picture of me in front of the White House in Washington D.C.

I own 119 healing time to reverse inner-self team fears.

My transcending light quest owned these realities.

TIP Δ - I lost all attachments and survived.

TIP Δ - I am not afraid to be alive in Pangaea.

TIP Δ - I own life is transcending and explore everything life has.

TIP Δ - I do not fear love, being in love, or rejection.

TIP Δ - I own child-like trust for new relationships.

This is Harpers Ferry, West Virginia the headquarters of the Appalachian Trail (AT). It is considered the AT trails halfway. Where is my human compass taking my journey?

I learned to disagree with the harmful idea of labels and one is better than another. Labels had me own I am less than human. Labeling others has them be less than human. Should everyone be labeled as small, regular, or large?

The only label anyone owns is human. A patient might own a label diagnosis appearing as permanent. The stigma of this diagnoses is not permanent. The near future holds cures for many illnesses. Some reading this book will live to be one-hundred and sixty.

My Human Compass's core values find an inner-self home.

All the Aspen trees along the mountains of Colorado are attached through a single root system. Humans are also attached to the oneness root of humanity. Each of us attaches to the roots of our one humanity tribe. I took the following picture of Aspen trees on a hike I did in the beautiful Rocky Mountains of Colorado. I hiked part of the Colorado Continental Divide Trail.

Stability-Healing Questions

How can diary entries of sad, fear, anger, and love help heal MHC?

How does diary entries of thankful and responsibility heal MHC?

Why would MHC own exaggerated fight or flight?

How does child-like trust heal MHC?

How does MHC own inner-self team stability?

How does the inner-self pyramid heal MHC?

How does patience help heal MHC?

Why does anger prevent MHC entry into the pyramid?

How do the diary entry questions heal MHC?

What is MHC thankful for and responsible for?

How did losing all attachments help heal MHC?

What are the stability messages MHC can own?

What keeps MHC out of Emergency Rooms?

How do the root connections of all humans to humanity heal MHC?

Chapter 15 Transcending Humanity Equality

Label Free Dan!
At The Womb
Babies Are Given
Gooey Labels Stuck
Pink Blue Blanket?
Shy Or Outgoing?
Bully Or Bullied?
Poor Or Rich?
Member Of This?
Member Of That?
Left Right Brained?
Jock Or Nerd?
Humans Sorted Into
Buckets Of Labels
Antiquated Wounding Labels!
Must Move Beyond
Labels Own Judgments
Everyone Is Transcending
Enrolled Into Humanity
No More Labels

I am labeled as male and others react to me based on this. I am labeled as male and others respond to me by this. I am labeled as being mid-life and others react to me based on this. Actions of others towards me can be based on these societal labels of physical characteristics seen in me. These labels can be seen as either negative or positive depending on another's life experiences and ancestral inheritance. Others react to me based on social status, weight, clothing, physical appearance, cleanliness, and the material possessions I own.

TIP Δ - No label defines who I am and where I am going.

My ownership of voice now validated, positive core values, set self-discipline, and my human compassion define me.

Everyone is living on earth for very brief periods of time. No one has time for giving or owning labels.

Life's TOO Short!

I am a stability-healing hero named My Human Compassion. I own no race. I own no social status. I own no gender.

I own human.

The major issue with being labeled as a victim, monster, good, evil, addict, and or in recovery is healers, support groups, and communities apply these label judgments to a human for a lifetime. A person getting this label applies this gooey brand to himself or herself for a lifetime.

TIP Δ – Transcending light vibrations owns no labels or judgments.

The clothing, weight, and cleanliness I wear say a lot. This can be so loud voice now heard words might not be heard at all. Labeling makes it harder to overcome judgments and heal. Those who suffer illness can own this label for a lifetime. Those labeled with an illness are seen as in constant recovery from a label. Labeling one as ill or in recovery owns judgment and shame. Owning a label is as if I live outside of humanity. I have heard of some being permanently labeled optimistic (positive) or pessimistic (negative). I find this to be harmful. Human labels of regular, large, or jumbo prevent healing.

I encourage trusted inner-influenced action based therapy for individuals suffering from any illness, addiction, abuse, and negative ancestral inheritance. My therapy experiences encouraged a series of labels imposed on me by society and healers. These are questions healers should use instead of forcing labels on others.

How is your daily well-being in your diary writings?
Do you have a job with meaning you love?
How stable are your relations with partner, friends, and family?
Do you own safety, acceptance, and stability?
Do you own needs?

I do not touch labels.

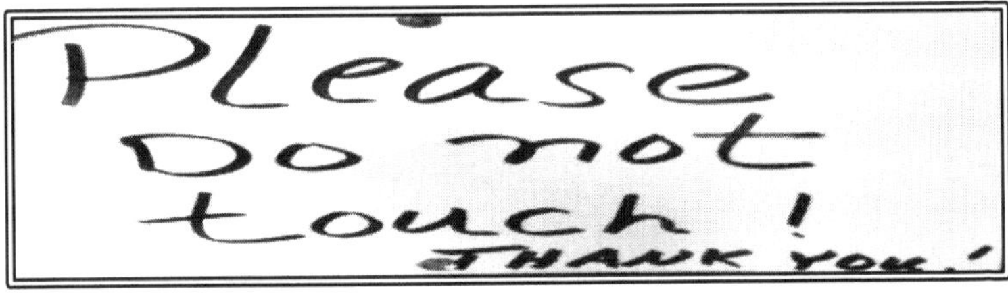

Each human is made of organs, bones, and skin. Labels push humanity apart instead of bringing us together. Labels divide humans up to be bark samples of different trees. I took this picture while visiting a ranger station at a Bronx New York City park.

Each human is from the same tree of life called humanity. What is going on in my well-being is not from labels.

I am motivated to own positive inner-self team changes. The years are going by so very fast. I must do what it takes to be alive-owning-now. Owning transcending humanity equality I go forward in my life letting my human compassion spring forth from my well-being to reach inner-self transcending so I can be a winner in my life.

No one is greater than another.

I took group therapy where everyone was introduced using a label a healer and medical manual gave him or her. A woman told tales supporting a label of a well-being as a victim. Another man labeled himself as an addict. Many group members were in permanent recovery. There are many oohs and ahs of sadness from others when these heart wrenchingly sad label introductions are made. This sympathy owns a huge negative reward to those owning and telling others of their well-being label. This sympathy to the one owning a negative label rewards a person and encourages them to own labels for a lifetime. I see nothing positive about labels.

TIP Δ – I, Voice Now Heard, introduce myself label free.

TIP Δ – I, Voice Now Heard, introduce myself as human.

The gooey labels of recovery, addiction, genetics, illness, and victimization can be forever stuck upon one's well-being with super glue. It is as if these labels can never be removed.

I cut labels to climb out of a dangerous hornet's nest of labels.

Transcending light vibrations doesn't label anyone as an addict, victim, or in recovery. Everyone owns inner-self home Pangea equally. It is my 3 Denver, Colorado bus ticket taking me to my inner-self home 3 = AUM well-being.

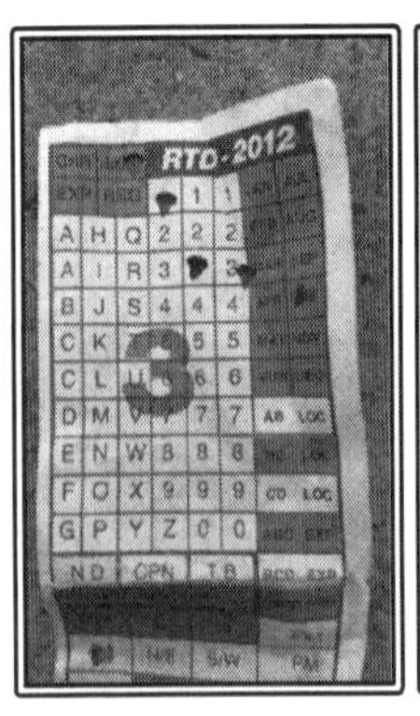

The transcending light vibrations need everyone to be healed. Flaws and mistakes are in our transcending equality template.

TIP Δ – I decide my identity outside of labels.
TIP Δ – I decide my identity using my positive core values.

Why place judgment labels on others or myself when it causes me to pay the highest price of losing my human identity?

Owning labels left my journey stuck in the wilderness.

There has been crisis in my life. A great gift to me is I learn to embrace healing with my twelve first nation-healing names.

TIP Δ – Stable-senses tools and owning positive actions.
TIP Δ – Inner-influenced actions and stability-healing diaries.
TIP Δ – I attach to people owning positive umbilical cords.
TIP Δ – My inner-self pyramid observes and stabilizes my moods.

Others depend on My Human Compassion. Others need my help, inspiration, hope, and charity. Humanity provides the trail map to healing each of us. I follow this trail map in Colorado.

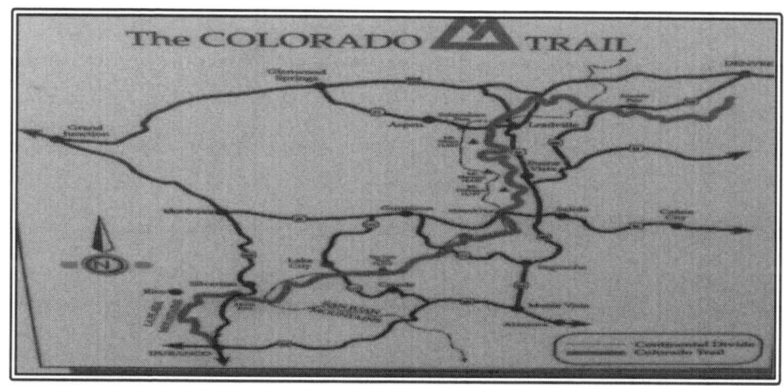

The transcending equality template has endured for ages before me and will continue on after my life. Humanity has endured a great deal of suffering and compassion. Humanity will survive!

TIP Δ – I am very happy when helping others and doing charity.
TIP Δ – I focus on how I can give healing first aid to others.

Life doesn't fit into any labels. Life is negative or positive. Life is happy or sad. Life is fair or unfair. Life is right or wrong. Life is good or bad.

TIP Δ – My life depends on my positive core values.
TIP Δ - I learned to enjoy my time alone and love my identity.

My hammock camping on the Appalachian Trail taught me the importance of learning how to heal, enjoy my alone time, and the importance of the Boy Scouts Motto "Be Prepared". This photo is my campsite in the Virginia Shenandoah National Park.

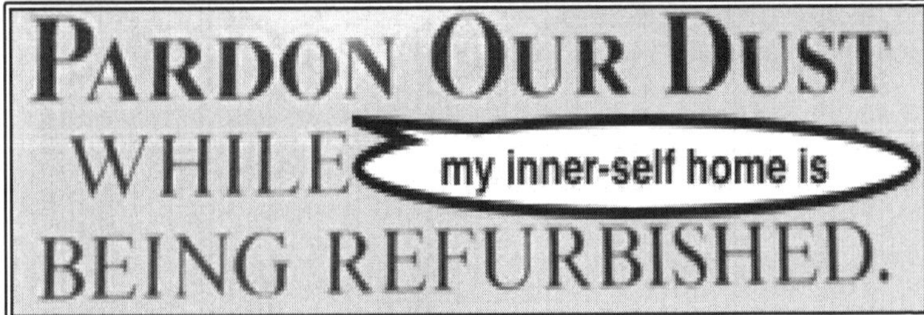

The light has changed in Midtown Atlanta Georgia. It is safe to go forward with humanity ridding labels. Lets continue up the stairs to visit more threes and learn how I broke my spell.

I move to compassionate freedom. One Love. One-Cord. One-Root. I am one with humanity pain, joy, and compassion. When my inner-self team platform gets closed due to shut down reboot I am never afraid to move to an open platform by saying, "I need help" to a stability-healing hero.

I learn to create a happily ever after inner-self home. Every day I shout and write out the following types of sayings. "I am my I am love." "I am my I am transcending!" "I am my I am protected!" These types of "I AM" statements help me transcend.

Trail along with me on how I learn to break my spell causing needless suffering. I become aware of the spell I am under. I know my spell originated from ancestral inheritance and experience after womb-healed birth. A hypnotist can put anyone into a spell. My years of looking glass-fears had me hypnotized. Anyone can be under a spell. I learn to break all spells so I own inner-self love.

Stability-Healing Questions

How can others predetermined ideas of MHC affect healing?

How does MHC owning that life is short heal?

How does MHC owning "only" the label of human heal?

How do societal labels hurt the healing of MHC?

How does transcending humanity equality heal MHC?

How does no humans on a pedestal help heal MHC?

How does MHC become a life winner?

How did group therapy help and hurt MHC?

How can inner-self meditations/prayers heal MHC?

Why are labels hurting humanity?

How does MHC refurbish the inner-self home?

How do "I AM" healing statements heal MHC?

Chapter 16 Break My Spell

Daniel Protects Danny
Alive-Owning-Now!
Life Is Transcending
Looking Glass Shattered!
I Compassionately Awaken!
Old Wounds Healed
Enlightened Universal Attached
Breaking My Spell
Owning Positive Ancestry
Boldly Walking Now
Transcending Equality Template
Inner-Self Team
Child-Adult-Parent
Danny-Dan-Daniel
Inner-Self Playful
Inner-Self Love
Voice Now Heard
Inner-Self Woman
Inner-Self Man
Others-Self Forgiven
Inner-Self Approval
My Human Compassion
Inner-Self Protected
Voice Now Validated
Compassion-Based Parent
Inner-Self Transcending
Get Your Things
MHC Takes Everyone
Inner-Self Home

Forgiveness is crucial to breaking my spell. There is no way to pick ancestors, parents, or siblings. I had few options about how others parented me during my childhood. Daniel is in the compassion-based parent stage.

TIP Δ - I forgive myself and others who failed to own my needs.
TIP Δ – I school others on evolutionary ways to heal.

School of Human Evolution and Social Healing.

One day in the 1990s I was traveling to the very small remote Isle of Wight situated off the coast of England. I was in a taxi and striking up conversation with the driver as I attempted to find my lodging for the night. Unknown to me this is not an island where one can easily find a hotel. The only places available are a few bed and breakfasts closing early.

Time stands still on this island as if it is stuck in the 1960s. This island brought back memories of my childhood. This is the place to go in order to find a town where every stranger is a friend. Striking up conversation I asked the driver if he met celebrities. I mentioned a few names. He said these words:

No I never heard of those people. Those people don't have squat to do with my life. Those celebrities do not help me with owning my needs. The people who matter are family and friends.

TIP Δ – Lots of people birth into the world and lots die out.

As we drove around attempting to find one of the few open bed and breakfast places, he offered his place for the night. What a compassionate offer.

I was drawn to spending the day on the Isle of Wight, why? It was about seeing another location few have seen. This was a new adventure to a new place with questions and answers to own.

TIP Δ – I alone am responsible for honest courageous work to heal.
TIP Δ – It is myself I accept with all of my flaws.

TIP Δ – It is myself I must forgive. Owning forgiveness to all others is my admission to healing.

I forgive my father for anger, abuse, guilt, shame, and blame.
I forgive my Mother for anger, abuse, guilt, shame, and blame.
I forgive bullies for anger, abuse, shame, and blame.
I forgive my siblings for rejection.
I forgive myself for anger, abuse, guilt, shame, blame, judgment, and rejection I owned for my inner-self team.

I forgive all who wounded me so I can get on a sled and ride all the way to my inner-self home. This picture was taken at the Great Sand Dunes National Park in Colorado. I loved sledding the dunes!

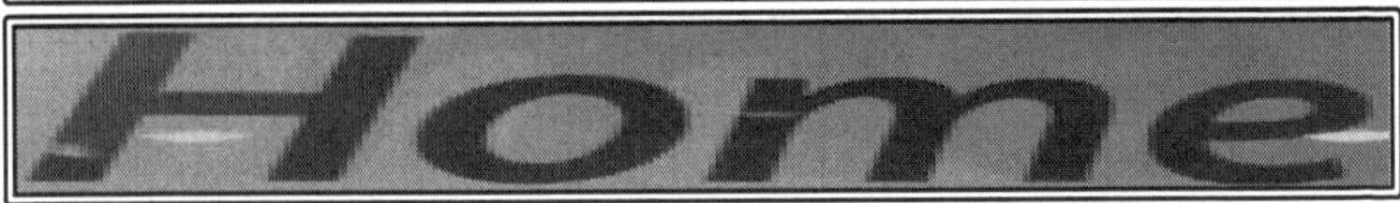

My inner-self team suffering transcends into compassion. Most of my life suffering is from my uniformed decisions. It is my compassion-based parent responsibilities when I look within for my stability. I explore new ways to heal. I am on the journey to be a great stability-healing hero.

TIP Δ – Transcending light vibrations own life truths with no judgments, no blame, no guilt, and no shame. The future is bright and challenges will be overcome. My diary helps me own stability.

I meet new people and learn new things to transcend compassion. I heal when I compassion-based parent my inner-self team. I own my responsibilities to transcend into maturity. I learn from what is going on inside of my inner-self home by carefully observing my well-being. I own a daily routine of active well-being listening. I learn all I can on healing.

I went to many Walter Cronkite School of Journalism lectures in Phoenix Arizona. I gained a lot of 333-compassion-based knowledge! Walter Cronkite is the best moral, ethical, and honest journalist's of all time. I took this picture near the lecture hall.

My transcending light quest brought on a painful argument to break my spell on the anniversary of my second oldest brother's death. Hyper-Love Forgiven blamed me for sending emails to people I should not have. I gave her access to my email account violating my set self-discipline. Hyper-Love Forgiven deleted many of my emails. She screamed at me, "I was revealing her private information without her permission."

I owned anger when she deleted my emails and violated my set self-discipline. I yelled back at her. Hyper-Love Forgiven face twisted in a rage I had not seen since I was fifteen when Angry Mother Forgiven owned this same rage. Slamming the laptop threatened Hyper-Love Forgiven. I lost safety, acceptance, and stability. Hyper-Love Forgiven and I owned spells of abuse. We should have walked away to own set self-discipline like these statues.

Her rage was as boundless as Angry Mother Forgiven. I had to own action. I dropped to the floor and got my body in a protective position. I crawled to the corner putting my arms over my head. My inner-self child cried out, "Please don't hurt me!"

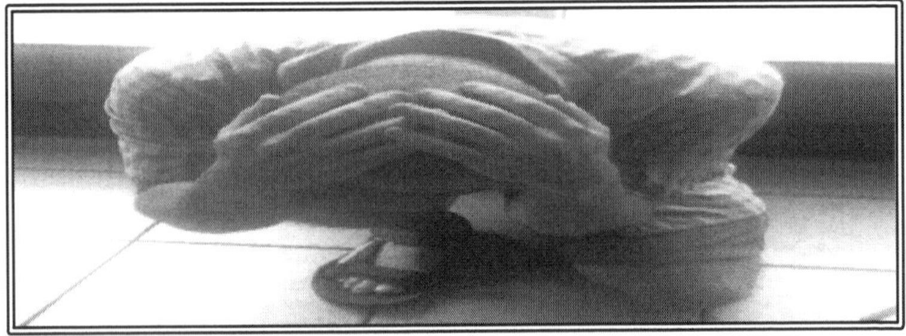

Seeing my submissive action Hyper-Love Forgiven calmed down and walked away. I was transported in a time machine thirty years ago to the age of fifteen. I was in the same Angry Mother Forgiven argument. As a child I was unable to set self-discipline. My inner-self parent Daniel protected inner-self child Danny. This broke my thirty-year spell and life went full circle. Daniel was now able to protect Dan in dangerous situations. This broke my spell with Angry Mother Forgiven. This argument was a way to heal my inner-self team. I own my inner-self team domestic crime prevention unit.

Hyper-Love Forgiven lacked stable-senses tools. I break my spell and I am closer to my mother. I owned my entire life based on a past spell. I often stopped relationships before they could transcend because I feared they would turn into the one with my parents. I deserve a partner who owns a stable well-being. I have a buffet of healing options. It is my responsibility to own healing working best for me.

TIP Δ – My unmet childhood needs are no longer important.
TIP Δ – I understand, define, and own my present needs.

I am the one living my life.
My life is my responsibility.

TIP Δ - I avoid negative ancestral messages and break my spell.
TIP Δ – My transcending light quest helped break my spell.
TIP Δ – My future relations will own compassion-based listening.
TIP Δ – My future relations will own well-being available.

TIP Δ – I found it best to relocate from where my spell was made.

TIP Δ – I can find a job in a new town and start over.

TIP Δ – I regain my child like trust to let healing arrive.

...you've arrived.

I own life-changing vows so I can own my healing. My vows support commitments to my positive core values. Vows allow me to sprout wings to be my own guardian angel. I made lots of mistakes. My errors enroll me in humanity. The angels help my journey.

With all of my mistakes I tried and failed so I might succeed one day. I embrace stability lessons learned. I made these most important vows to my inner-self team so I would not repeat old wounding routines. These vows own positive umbilical cord relationships and find me a meaningful job I love. My transcending light quest took a Harpers Ferry turning point in my hike across the country. I moved to Colorado with a friend.

Harpers Ferry turning point

My transcending light quest was a university of great knowledge. This picture was taken on a break on my hike from Harpers Ferry West Virginia into the beautiful Shenandoah Valley area of Virginia.

I never knew what I would see on my transcending light quest. I am in a downtown Phoenix park and I saw a fire thrower. I can see all of our shared ancestors in transcending light vibrations.

Grab your inner-self team. MHC is taking you inner-self home!

If you get lost.

TIP Δ – I own inner-self love to avoid getting lost.

This is a message my compassion-based parent gives my inner-self child Danny, "I will always love you, protect you, and I will never leave you. I cannot make it alone. I am the one who owns your healing. I am the stability-healing hero you need." It is a Happy New Year for the healing 201 ॐ brings humanity.

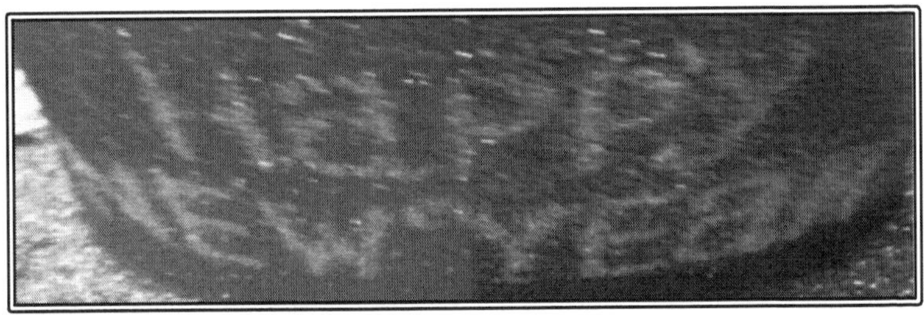

A picture of a tree in a New York City Park reminds of every third-eye intertwined in transcending light vibrations and humanity.

Stability-Healing Questions

Who are the important people mattering to MHC?

How does forgiveness break the spell MHC was under?

How does being a seeker and teacher help heal MHC?

What stability lessons learned does MHC own?

How can MHC own a voice now validated?

How does MHC compassion-based parent?

How did MHC break a spell?

How did the MHC inner-self parent protect MHC inner-self child?

Who does owning responsibility help MHC transcend into maturity?

How does the MHC inner-self team heal?

How can MHC own all elements of the inner-self home?

What does MHC write in this diary about breaking a spell?

How does MHC keep from getting lost on life's journey?

What enrolls MHC into humanity?

Chapter 17 Inner-Self Transcending

Dan-Danny-Daniel
Now Owning Vows
Forever Self-Stabilized
Safety, acceptance, and stability
Compassion-Based Listening
119-Reversing Fears
Taking Positive Actions
Negative Cords Cut
Positive Cords Attached
Moving Life Forward
Alive-Owning-Now
Honest Courageous Work
Embracing Life Changes
Transcending Light Vibrations
Stability-Healing Heroes
Positive Support Groups
Anger To Compassion
Compassion-Based Parent
Danny-Dan-Daniel
Child-Adult-Parent
Well-Being Transcending
Inner-Self Team
Take Me Home!

There are many life-changing vows I must make with friends, family, partners, community, and myself. The following vows, questions, and answers help me own an inner-self transcending.

TIP Δ – How can well-being availability own my needs?
TIP Δ – How does compassion-based listening own my needs?

The Boy Scouts could have another badge for anyone spending weeks and months surviving on their own in the trails. It could be called the pterodactyl badge.

What makes me never-give-up to make it to the next day?
How do I avoid others trespassing on my set self-discipline?

My inner-self team can get flooded with stimuli. My well-being might go to exaggeration, fantasy, extreme positivity, or extreme negativity but I learn to own stability. I own stability lessons learned from my past. I learn important vows working best for me.

A vow might be to own independence.
A vow might be to start a new job or end a current one.
A vow might be to go back to school to learn a new career.
A vow might be to end a relationship or start a new one.
A vow might be to move to a new geographical location.
A vow might be to end a business or start a new one.

TIP Δ - I own free thinking to determine my unique vows.

My vows patrol my inner-self team well-being.

I do not block my journey to inner-self transcending.

TIP Δ – These are daily diary questions I ask.

What can I do to help my inner-self team own my needs?
What proactive things can I do to continue healing as I age?
What can I help humanity survive in 201 ॐ and beyond?

TIP Δ - My life-changing vows move me beyond my past.

I vow to own positive core values for inner-influenced actions.
I vow to own set self-discipline for my inner-self team.
I vow to own human civil rights needs for others and myself.
I vow to own forgiveness for others instantly.
I vow to own the replacement of anger with compassion.
I vow to own well-being availability.
I vow to own compassion-based listening.

Similar to wedding vows, these are vows I must own every day from rising up in the morning to going to sleep at night. I write my name and my vows in sand. This is taken at the Great Sand Dunes National park in Colorado

I vow to own a life is transcending approach to living.
I vow to own a first nation-healing approach.
I vow to own a permanent cut to negative umbilical cords.
I vow to own positive umbilical cord relationships.
I vow to own child-like trust to love without fear.
I vow to own my life with 119-reversing of all fears.
I vow to own humanity super heroes with no labels.
I vow to own my life as a stability-healing hero.
I vow to own stable-senses tools and positive actions.
I vow to own daily rock bottom ownership and rise up.
I vow to remain inside the inner-stability pyramid.
I vow to own my life purpose as a hero healer advocate.
I vow to be the best human civil rights leader I can be.

I declare these life-changing vows on March 3, 201 ॐ .
My life-changing vows enroll me into humanity.
These vows are how I reach for the stars in my future success!

I own everyone must own needs. I own relationships own love with mutual compassion. I own life is not fair and my organizations do the honest courageous hard work to make life fairer. Transcending light vibrations tell me to never-give-up.

I own stability lessons learned to not repeat ancestral mistakes. I own tools to own a healing inner-self home. These vows allow my inner-self team compassions to shine. Welcome to My Human Compassion. I am happy our paths crossed.

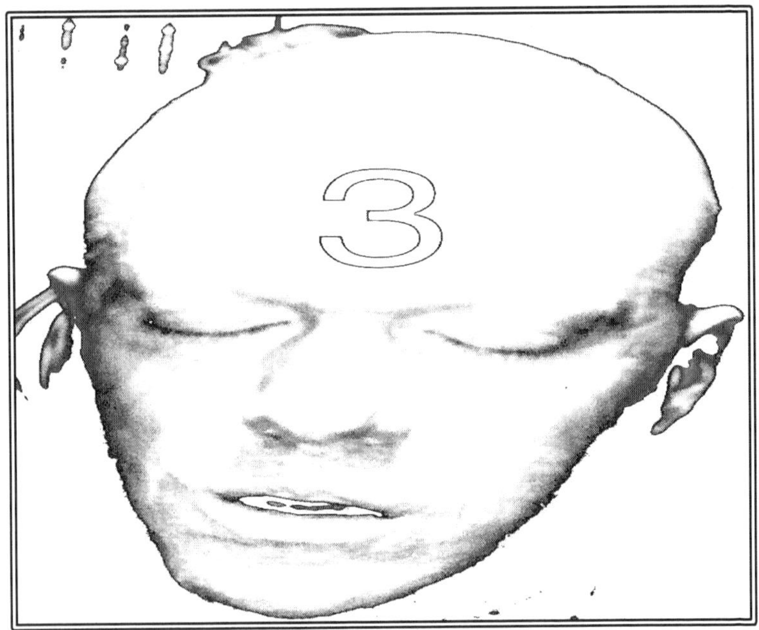

At times I felt I wanted to stop changes occurring in my transcending light vibrations. For years I did the same routines day in and day out even if they were self-defeating. This was my wasted attempt to stop change. My transcending light quest took me outside those routines. It taught me how to love transcending.

TIP Δ – My routines from the 1960s to 2011 prevented healing.
TIP Δ – My transcending light quest of 2011 to 2013 owned healing.

Now is the time in my life to own healing. New healing events, people, and places will reveal themselves. New healing tools and education will come my way.

TIP Δ – I go beyond my usual social boundaries.
TIP Δ – I live outside comfort zone and negative routines.

I own the vital importance to be thankful for everything I have. I shared well-being available talking in my diary. It was a surprise to learn how lovely life can be when I learned how to own safety, acceptance, and stability. This is a memorial at the state capital in Phoenix Arizona reminding me of how veteran stability heroes give us freedom while sacrificing their needs and sometimes their life.

TIP Δ – I vow to change my life to what it must be.
TIP Δ – I focus on what inner-influenced actions I must do.

I write in my diary the deeply buried well-being statuses. I tell these to my stability-healing heroes so I may swim away from the deep end of my old wounds. This was taken at the Phoenix Arizona Young Men's Christian Association (YMCA). I stayed here to complete this diary on March 2013.

My inner-self team owns set self-discipline restricted entrance. This was taken at a hospital in Atlanta Georgia where I got the medication that healed my bleeding colon.

I set up a clear communication plan and contractual relationships with my trusted healers to own my unique healing goals. I am careful about the money I spend on healing. I don't waste hard earned money on healers, therapy, and medications proving to be unhelpful. I do what it takes to feed my family and find the healers who promote inner-self influenced healing.

Quitting therapy and firing healers can be difficult. The umbilical cord of gurus, therapists, healers, clergy, and healers create is difficult to cut. I consult my inner-self love, stability-healing heroes, positive support groups before quitting my current healing options.

TIP Δ - Healers might try to influence me to visit them long past the time when I need their help. There are free or low cost healers.

I was going to ride the rails in Atlanta Georgia to my next destination. My inner-self protected said a decisive no. This is a picture of me letting the rail cars go by without jumping on one.

As I complete this diary I am at the same age as my father when he owned mid-life crisis. This is my stability-healing diary. I do not see myself as a citizen of any country. My Human Compassion is in the Pangaea community. My passport is stamped citizen of Pangaea. Transcending light vibrations and inner-self love heal me.

All life negative or positive events are for a greater purpose. It gave me greater compassion to shape my future. Beautifully polished gems are from centuries of stone grinding against stone. Any life owns suffering similar to stone grinding against stone.

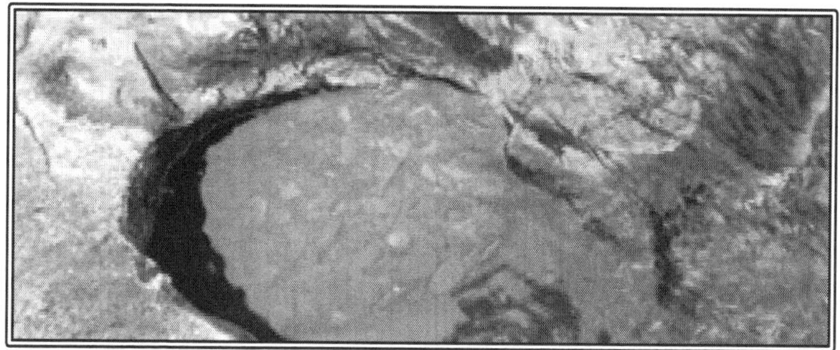

I am a much better person for my life sufferings. These grindings of suffering transcend into compassion. These alter my inner-self team into becoming a beautiful gem.

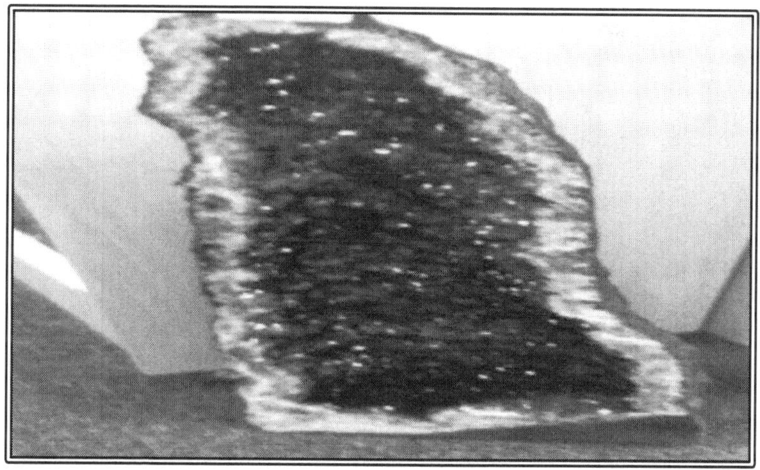

Transcending light vibrations heals us every day. Every inner-self team is a beautiful unique gem. I took this picture at the Tucson Arizona Sonoran Desert museum. This is a great place to visit.

When each of us is born, our Mother and father are **"seemingly all powerful"** from a child's point of view. The life is transcending approach is parents nor any other are all powerful. I created a first nation-healing renaming ceremony so my ancestors own accurate first nation-healing names.

I rename Angry Mother Forgiven to Mother Loves Child.
I rename Abusive Father Forgiven to Father Loves Child.
I rename all of my siblings to Brother Loves Brother.
I rename all past bullies to Humans Loving Humanity.

First nation-healing renaming ceremonies own myself, Mother Loves Child, Father Loves Child, and all Ancestors with giant love.

TIP Δ – These are messages Mother Loves Child owns for me.

Danny-Dan-Daniel! I love you and I accept you completely.
Danny-Dan-Daniel! I allow you to set self-discipline with me.
Danny-Dan-Daniel! I am your compassion-based parent.
Danny-Dan-Daniel! I validate and hear your voice now heard.
Danny-Dan-Daniel! I support your core values.
Danny-Dan-Daniel! I am the stability-healing hero you need.
Danny-Dan-Daniel! I am well-being available.
Danny-Dan-Daniel! I am compassion-based listening to you.
Danny-Dan-Daniel! I will always support you.
Danny-Dan-Daniel! I will move you from crisis to stability.
Danny-Dan-Daniel! I give you safety, acceptance, and stability.
Danny-Dan-Daniel! I am here to help you own your needs.
Danny-Dan-Daniel! I own my human compassion for you.
Danny-Dan-Daniel! I support you in your life-changing vows.
Danny-Dan-Daniel! I am your stability-healing hero.

TIP Δ – These are messages Father Loves Child owns for me.

Danny-Dan-Daniel! I love you and I accept you completely.
Danny-Dan-Daniel! I allow you to set self-discipline with me.
Danny-Dan-Daniel! I help move you from crisis to stability.
Danny-Dan-Daniel! I support your positive core values.
Danny-Dan-Daniel! I am your stability-healing hero.
Danny-Dan-Daniel! I listen and validate your voice now heard.
Danny-Dan-Daniel! I am compassion-based listening to you.
Danny-Dan-Daniel! I am well-being available.
Danny-Dan-Daniel! I give you safety, acceptance, and stability.
Danny-Dan-Daniel! I am your compassion-based parent.
Danny-Dan-Daniel! I support your life-changing vows.
Danny-Dan-Daniel! I am your stability-healing hero.

I hope everyone renames parents, relatives, bullies, or anyone else causing old wounds. Renaming heals and fades away old negative messages and events. These new names are based on compassion and forgiveness. In doing this renaming ceremony I and my descendants own stable ancestry/descendents.

TIP Δ – I went from owning old wounds to learning how to own a healed adult life. Everything has gone full circle in my life.

I evaluate my inner-self team for what my core values are. I own the freedom to an existence owning the now. I own an awakened first nation-healing life. I own my constant continual healing changes while aging. I own inner-self child-like joy and trust in everyday living. I can change my aging life outlook back to a womb-healed baby reality no matter my age.

If I am well-being unstable or in a crisis I never-give-up! I got to make it through this tough day. There is another better-healed day to be owned - beyond this one. I will own my tomorrow. Things will get better and I will walk beyond chaos and crisis. I will make it to tomorrow and never-give-up!

I am never afraid to say I need help to trusted healers. I am not afraid to contact stability-healing heroes or call 911. The actions I own decide my results. A new day is an opportunity to own my life as looking glass shattered.

TIP Δ – Everyone faces life challenges, suffering, and illness.

Doing and creating my transcending light quest transformed my life. I own stability awareness and advocacy.

TIP Δ – My greatest charity gives others a meaningful job they love.

As I go forward in life; I permanently cut negative umbilical cords. I attach positive umbilical cords to stability-healing heroes. I took the following picture on the floor of the New York City Subway system. How do I own a stability-healing hero way to live?

I attach to transcending light vibrations, inner-self love, and humanity. I hope for long living stability in the future of humanity.

I faced crisis and overcame. I enact compassion to my inner-self team and stop judging myself. I fade away old wounds into our transcending light vibrations.

I am free.
I am whole.
I am loved.

It is easy to finish reading self-help, complete healing seminars, and own inspiration to own change. Own the can do will do desire to make positive changes now. A few days go by and it is easy for me to fall into old routines.

How do I stop old wounding routines?
How do I make the most out of my diary?

TIP Δ – I sign a contract to own life-changing vows.

TIP Δ – I write vows down in my stability-healing diaries.

TIP Δ – I memorize vows and refer back to them daily.

TIP Δ – I write down daily well-being updates.

TIP Δ – I reveal my diaries to the stability-healing heroes I trust.

Suppose I have a stroke and survive. A healer says another stroke will come unless I change routines creating the first one. I must own actions to reduce stress, stop smoking, and change my diet. If I learned from the stroke, I own proactive actions. If I learn nothing then I will change nothing. I then own everything happening to me. Another stroke. My life involves trying, failing, and success. May everyone own a happy ॐ New Year!

The next time I fall in love fall in love with the most important person in my life, which is my inner-self team. I love my inner-self team before I can love others. Inner-self love has me walk a healed journey paved with stars. I took this picture of my shadow and *Looking Glass Shattered* on Hollywood Boulevard California.

Stability-Healing Questions

How does MHC stop old wounding routines?

How do the diary never-give-up approaches heal MHC?

What well-being wounds did MHC bury?

What daily questions and answers must MHC think about?

How does first nation-healing renaming ceremonies heal MHC?

How does MHC own safety, acceptance, and stability?

How does MHC choose positive healers?

What are the MHC life-changing vows?

How can MHC improve upon life-changing vows?

How do the MHC diary never-give-up approaches heal?

What first nation-healing names does MHC use to heal old wounds?

How is becoming a beautiful gem healing for MHC?

How does signing a contract to own vows help heal MHC?

How does MHC own alive-owning-now?

Chapter 18 Our Next Steps

It is March 201 ॐ and my first transcending light quest diary is complete. This has been a living breathing document for the last three years. Everything I did on my transcending light quest went against what was expected.

Go to work in a cube.
Have a family.
Get a morgue toe tag.

I met so many on the trails, in the cities, wilderness, and hostels. I would show up in a new town or trail with no plan. My inner-self team was child-like trustingly available to our transcending light vibrations. I had no idea what I was doing other than completing this diary. My transcending light quest brought the idea of home and homeless to me. A symbol of home is two partners embracing. This was taken at the Denver art museum.

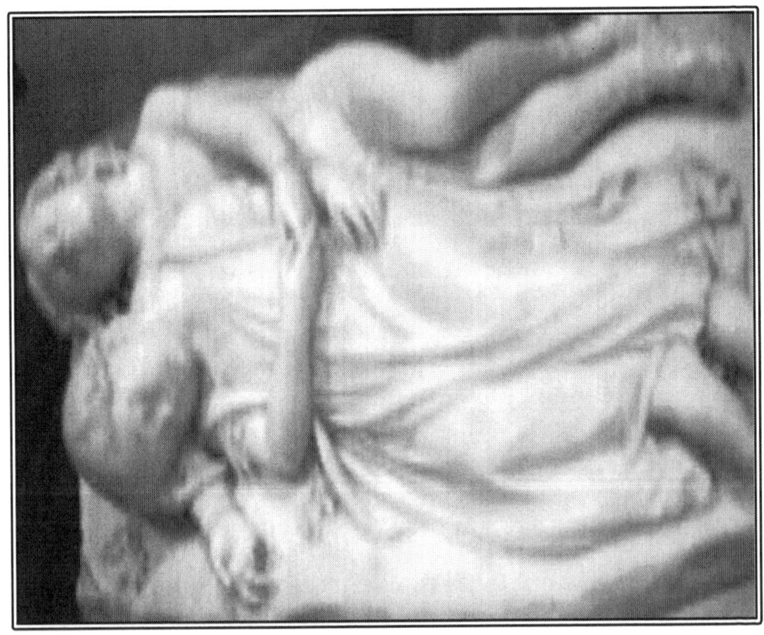

I discovered new healing products on my transcending light quest.

HEALER PRODUCTS

TIP Δ – This is a contract I sign with healers.

What is your plan to heal my inner-self team?
How do you focus on inner-influenced actions to heal?
What education and tools do you own for healing?
What is your motivation for being a healer?
What are your examples of healing successes and failures?
How is set self-discipline used in our healing sessions?
How do you use compassion-based healing?
How do you use well-being available talking?
What are our weekly and monthly contractual healing goals?
What are your tests to decide when our healing ends?
What free services and charity do you give back to our community?
How are you qualified to be a stability-healing hero?
Are you certified to heal me as a human or as a junk car?

TIP Δ – Umbilical cord cutting ceremony.
TIP Δ – I write these words in my diary.

<Insert name> I thank you for our <insert relationship>.
I cut our cord due to <abuse, death, rejection, and or etc.>.
I forgive <insert name> for the negative cord relationship.
I gained stability lessons learned from you and I move on.
I fade away negative messages into transcending light vibrations.
I write the relationship's negative messages onto fire-safe paper.
I burn sage in a fire-safe bowl.
I take the umbilical cut writings and burn them with the sage.
I write positive relationship messages on biodegradable paper.
I place these writings in moving water (i.e. river, ocean, etc.).

TIP Δ – I say the following words out loud.

The negative umbilical cord is cut forever.
Out of sage ashes I own inner-self team healed.
I rid all pain and anger against you.
I will never see you again <insert name>.
I own all positive nurturing events and messages you gave me.
Life suffering gave me challenges and I am better for that.
I forgive you and I own my human compassion for you.

I release you <insert name> on this date ____________.

I permanently umbilical cut our relationship leaving no trace.

TIP Δ – I meditate this prayer to transcending light vibrations.

Let transcending light vibrations go in me.
Let transcending light vibrations heal me.

Heal my crown chakra.
Heal my third-eye chakra.
Heal my throat chakra.
Heal my heart chakra.
Heal my solar plexus chakra.
Heal my sacral chakra.
Heal my root chakra.
Thank you for my healing!

I owned lots of beautiful threes when I ordered this tea at a local coffee shop in Phoenix Arizona.

The tea costs 3 dollars.
The tea takes 3 minutes to steep.
The tea owns 3 scoops.
The Internet Security code is 31313.

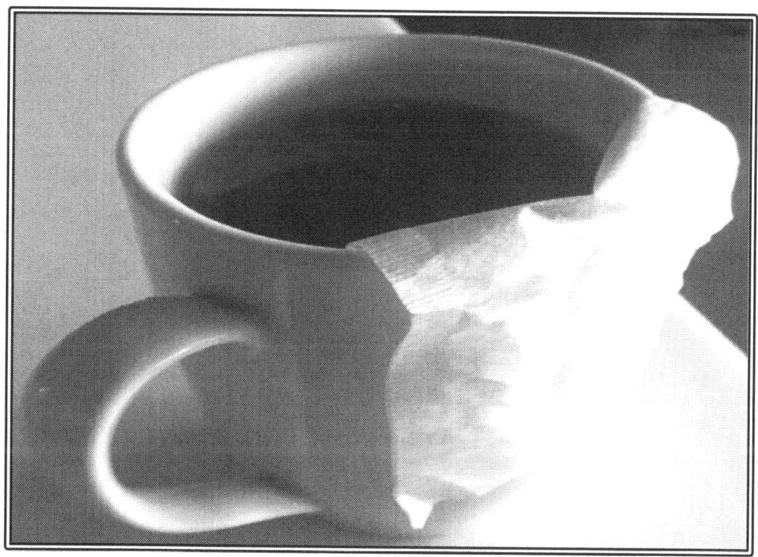

TIP Δ – Healing party extravaganza setup.

I dress in loose fitting relaxed comfortable clothes or pajamas best representing how my inner-self child needs to be.
I change my hair and clothing to look like my inner-self child.
I get in a relaxed position by sitting on a comfortable sofa or bed.
I go to a room owning safety, acceptance, and stability.
I use stability-healing diary writings for this ceremony.
I eat a nurturing meal my parents would make.
I hold a huggable healing hero stuffed toy with a photo of my Mother on it and another with a photo of my father on it.
My huggable healing hero toy owns nurturing motherly love.
My huggable healing hero toy owns positive fatherly love.
I write using well-being availability.
I write in my diary all childhood needs not met.

TIP Δ – Healing Party Extravaganza individual healing.

I own womb healings my huggable healing hero toys give.
I hug the huggable healing hero toys as long as necessary.
I show well-being availability of crying and shouting out anger, sadness, abuse, fear, hurt, and or love to these huggable toys.
I use these toys to rid old negative events and messages.
I own umbilical cord cut ceremonies with parents as needed.

A healing party extravaganza relaxes and heals my well-being.

TIP Δ – Healing Party Extravaganza group healing.

I own my huggable healing hero toys to a support group.
The leaders and participants sign contractual healer agreements.
I am well-being available about what my needs are.
I am safe to hug, cry, and yell to group members and huggable toys.
I discuss past compassion-based listening missed out on.
I discuss past well-being availability missed out on.
I write down the actions I need for this ceremony.

Huggable healing hero toys stabilize our inner-self home. Every one is here to stabilize and support each other's inner-self team.

On my travels in Phoenix Arizona I found an organization going around neighborhoods putting positive vibrational words of hope, peace, and love on urban fences. This helps inspire and motivate others for healing. Pangaea streets are full of love and compasion!

Let the compassionate transcending light vibrations breath healing life into you, your ancestors, and your descendants. Now I can let my inner-self love bloom.

Bless the AUM sound vibrational beats transcending light vibrations! The 333-beats and AUM rhythm of life are my inner-self home!

I awaken all the far reaches of my well-being. Each one of 7.2 billion falls in love with themselves! I am looking forward to meeting you on humanity trails. Mount Kilimanjaro in Tanzina Africa or Telluride Colorado?

Stability-Healing Questions

Why does MHC go against what is expected?

What is one of the MHC symbols of home?

How did ideas of home and homeless deeply affect MHC?

How does owning a healer contract heal MHC?

How can the guidelines of a healer contract heal MHC?

Why is it important for MHC to be able to fire a healer?

Why is it important for MHC to test a healer?

How does contractual goal setting help heal MHC?

How does writing and saying a cord cut ceremony heal MHC?

How does an individual healing party extravaganza heal MHC?

How does a group healing party extravaganza help heal MHC?

How does huggable healing hero toys individual therapy heal MHC?

How does huggable healing hero toys group therapy heal MHC?

How do huggable healing hero toys give MHC womb-healed?

Chapter 19 Pay It Forward

I am prepared to help humanity own a winning journey.

TIP Δ – I heal my inner-self team so I heal humanity.

When I met someone on my travels I mentioned I am completing a diary combining memoirs, self-help, transcending, personal transformation, poems, songs, photos, and much more. I was asked if it had recipes so I decided to add my favorite one.

Two slices of gluten-free pumpernickel bread.
Add organic sugar-free peanut butter to slices.
Add sugar-free organic honey to slices.
Add sugar-free organic hummus.
I wash it down with sugar-free organic green tea.

Everyone is on a journey to own inner-self transcending in this life or the next. It's easy to forget as external influences, technology, metallic clanking machines, non-stop streaming of terror, war, and pop culture overwhelms us. Yet transcending is always waiting to attach with my third-eye cord anytime I am ready. Every time I see the number three whether on a bill, bus number, or in the current time I am reminded of the healing of our universal compassion.

When I camped in Colorado at 5,258 feet I saw a view of the stars I never imagined. Brilliant bright smears of stars on backgrounds revealing countless galaxies. It is comforting to know this is the same light my ancestors lived in.

I traveled through many towns drifting in and out. I own a looking glass shattered life to make healing happen. Through my trying, failing, trying, and failing I survived. These experiences transcend me to own greater compassion. I want to help create new healing clinics and shelters. I cannot do this alone I need your help.

TIP Δ – Pay it forward owns the healing we need.

I am thankful for the people, adventures, and things in my life. In the present and future I provide stability-healing advocacy. Pay it forward faces challenges ahead yet its goal is to own positive changes based on compassion.

I need well-being available and transcending entertainment. I need stories about stability-healing heroes. Everyone needs permanent political changes our womb-brith guaranteed equal human civil rights guarantees. I created www.pokethedog.net to own greater attention to healing changes. The dog is a metaphorical symbol of current political and healthcare systems changes humanity must make. Many dogs enjoy their daily routines without change.

When I pay it forward I am prepared to heal humanity. I own 119-fearlessnesss on my journey to healing. Pay it forward owns increased liberty, justice, equality, freedom, and compassion into building humanities positive changes.

Shall I tread lightly?
Shall I own permanent everlasting footprints?

I visited hostels meeting hundreds of new friends along the way. I learned stories of humanity and gained friendships. This is my story surviving unknown cities, wilderness, and people. As I traveled first nation-healing vibrated throughout my transcending.

TIP Δ – These are visionary pay it forward solutions to heal.

My goal with MHC and pay it forward is to inspire and motivate others to create for-profit companies and non-profit organizations to own healing for Pangaea communities. I created a website called www.pokethedog.net to own positive changes.

I see myself as a go to person in supporting current and new healing organizations. MHC organizations are incubators in creating new healing organizations. I will be on the board of directors of these agencies to guide, inspire, and motive leaders to stay focused on their mission charter.

I met a lot of great leaders on my transcending light quest who need support and a push in the directions to make their dreams into reality. I help leaders, Chief Executive Officers, and Board Of Directors to stay on the ethical trail.

A domestic violence shelter protects families. Shelters provide needs including food, childcare, housing, jobs, and counseling. There is zero tolerance for any abuse. Shelters are doing and achieving the healing of humanity. I have new ideas on shelters we can create together.

Being human born, I own the same equal human civil rights to succeed as anyone. We no longer own first world, second world, or third. Everyone owns one-world Pangaea humanity.

Pangaea occupy movement's reminds each everyone to own equal human civil rights. The word of 2012 was occupied. The words of 201 are compassion and inner-self love.

Moses originally had three tablets. He dropped one. What do you want to be this is the one that said, "When everyone starts believing we are in end of days its not true." "We are actually in a time of wondrous healing!" It is understandable that Moses would be dropping tablets. Consider that he was unstable, starving, lacking water, and those tablets were very heavy! It was all he could do to be able to carry two tablets let alone three.

Some believe humanity is headed into end of days. I disagree. I believe healing is sweeping across every hill, valley, and mountaintop. We are in healing days and MHC is here to help.

On my travels across the country I was on the Tennessee River. Across from me was a long abandoned hospital leaking toxins into the ground water. Trash floated by and I smelled the stench of death. I greeted a fellow first-nation friend. He wore a hospital discharge band on his wrist with a label of brain instability. I told him of how I had seen a vision of a great healer on a horse. He said, "This proves our collective humanity is headed towards healing".

I hope everyone owns a looking glass shattered life.
Congratulations on graduating from this diary.

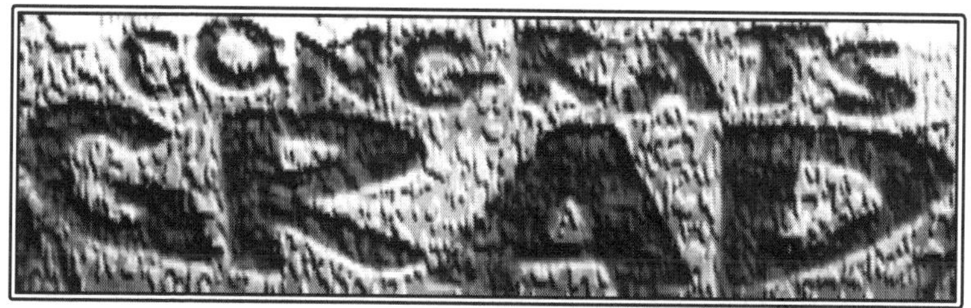

TIP Δ – Life truths are now happening across Pangaea.

We are going back to the ideals of tribal living. They say the rate of global warming increases super storms. These storms own a need for nimble tribal type governments.

Hurricane Ilene in the state of Vermont overwhelmed government authorities tasked with providing food, shelter, and clothes to those devastated families. I took it upon MHC charity in Stowe to donate clothing, food, and toys to start a charity for relief. I was faced with resistance by local business for trying to turn Stowe into a distribution center for charitable relief. Those businesses did not want their town to be the base of operations for this help.

We cannot depend on government or self-centered greedy businesses to fix absolute devastations brought from super storms. It is up to each individual to pick up the rocks, stones, and downed trees to clean up our cities. I nee my future children into a healed humanity. How can we heal veteran stability heroes?

How can we keep Sensory and Veterans heroes from homelessness?

How can we heal sensory stability heroes?

I go forward owning my never-give-up approaches. Through questions and answers I and humanity heal. MHC 119-fearlessness reverses 911 fears. We work together as stability-healing heroes. Let's heal Pangaea for every child and all descendants. I own a voice now validated to say how my well-being is doing.

I want to create a program similar to Alcoholic Anonymous (AA). Sensory stability heroes get support to continue maintaining their well-being with stabilizing medications. This program is known as Medications Anonymous (MA). These programs can exist in every city. Visionary solutions create positive changes for humanity.

Everything is transcending light vibration. The food I eat, the music I hear, and the events I attend. It is the laughter, the joy, the hot, the cold, the senses, and my moods.

All of this is transcending me into owning healed. Different vibrations heal different chakras. I did not have to jump out of an airplane, fall out of a raft, or hike fourteen thousand feet tall mountains. All I have to do is attach with the love of our shared transcending light vibrations. Each of us is apart of this loving flow. It is the energy all around us at all times.

Many things heal old wounds. There is music, visualizations, compassion, charity, life, friends, and love. I could finish the diary when I discovered the true value of the numbers 333. Anyone can become a transcending champion. I follow 3 steps to own healed!

TIP Δ – I seek greater truths and teach those truths to others.

TIP Δ – I, compassion-based parent, am a seeker and teacher.

TIP Δ – I motivate others to create organizations that heal Pangaea.

When I meet a homeless person, I wonder at what point in their life they went downhill. Age twelve, eighteen, twenty-seven, or fifty-one? What caused them to reach rock bottom without rising up? Were their stability-healing heroes available to help them? When did they give up on being among the living? I enjoy attending and giving lectures on how to heal. These are the topics I enjoy lecturing on.

Some say humanity might appear unreliable and their views might own wide acceptance. Those who say this have never met all seven point two billion humans. Is there basis for trusting humanity? Are there truths to humanity owning unreliability?

We can make assumptions based on media and entertainment as to our current well-being of humanity.

The issue is lack of knowledge regarding details of our times. Assumptions are made based on misunderstanding of the needs and true compassion of humanity.

The results confirm humanity can do nothing but gain from an increase of transcending light quest knowledge. Everyone can go out and meet as many fellow tribal members as possible.

The more individual transcending light quests we make the more we increase the truthful evidence yes humanity can be trusted and it is mostly compassionate. It is spreading human civil rights among the people on earth to own peace. Each of our unique transcending journeys defines humanity.

For humanity I sing and dance to song. Humanity is stronger than strong and mightier than mighty. Humanity, you deliver peace, love, and compassion. I anoint the earth with dance to show my love for humanity.

The vast majority of sensory stability heroes with brain instability are not cruel. A majority of heroes own fear and are unable to own needs. They lack tools to own stability. I teach stability.

The news creates negative stigma against heroes.
The news needs to state cruel people do cruel acts.
The news needs to state compassionate people do kind acts.
All brain instabilities are not the same.
News reports horrific crimes done by unstable people.
These stories are negative stigma to all with brain instability.
New gun control laws are not the solution.

People owning brain instability can be viewed as laughable for the strange actions they do. Others might see them as hopeless and doomed. I created this diary as a platform to own greater awareness on creating new proactive programs.

Free and or low cost well-being stabilizing medications save lives. My Human Compassion needs to help clean up the news.

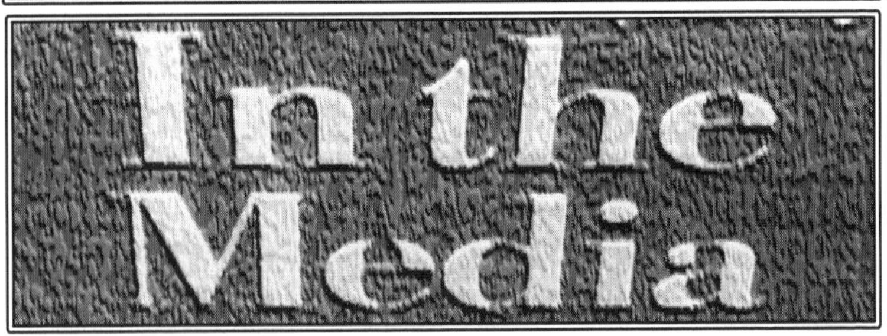

TIP Δ – After any violence, the news must ask these questions.

Has this person owned a lifetime of stability or instability?
Has this person had access to well-being stabilizers?
Has this person been supported by stability-healing heroes?
What proactive things could have prevented this crime?

How can society share well-being stabilizers to those in need?
Did this person eat nutritional foods owning stability?

TIP Δ – Government and communities can do more to give easy access to medications and nutrition owning stability. This will save lives. A vast majority of humanity is compassionate and I never let the media or entertainment looking glass fog this life truth.

Think of any number. Add a zero to the end representing the neutrally clear enlightened womb-healed compassion. Double this number – this represents every unique transcending journey. Add six to the number, which turns anger to compassion. Take half of this number, which has us in the transcending realm. Then remove the number started with (symbolizing death).

TIP Δ – The remaining answer is always 3 = ॐ compassion

This is the site of the July 2012 Aurora Colorado theater tragedy. My Human Compassion leads candle lighting compassion-based awareness events. My transcending light quest proved humanity is mostly made of 3 = ॐ compassion and it is safe to go outside.

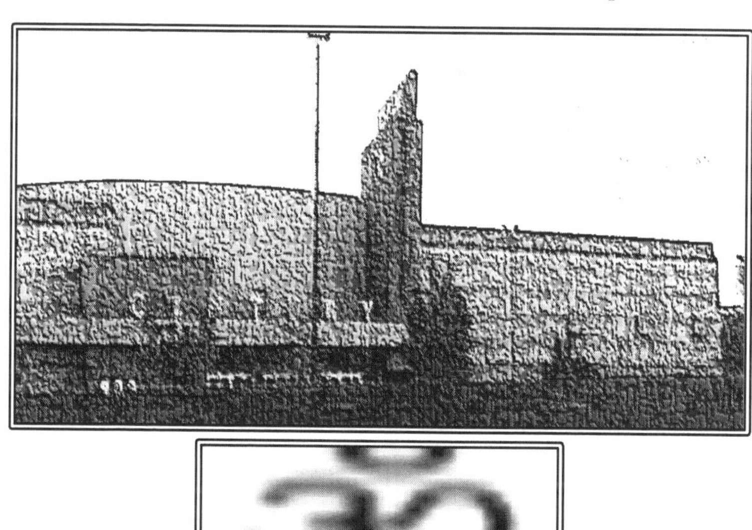

Out of the ashes of crisis emerges compassion.

TIP Δ – First nation-healing is my inner-self sanctuary of healing.

Humanity loosened my chains and set me free. Humanity saved my life countless times.

Thank you Transcending Light Vibrations.
Thank you Humanity.

We provide methods of raising personal compassion felt by every human in the company of shared ancestral humanity toward the ongoing trustworthy equation of humanity.

Humanity is the splendor and the beauty. Oh how we love your healing power. Humanity and transcending light vibrations picks us up and turns everyone around.

I took the "find the hero in you" picture from the side of a Red Cross van doing a blood drive on Arizona State University campus. I took the picture of myself in a mirror at the Phoenix public library.

I praise humanity and transcending light vibrations to carry each of us through storms, wars, and chaos. I look lovingly at my inner-self team in the mirror and say, "I own inner-self love, I own the stability-healing hero within, I love transcending light vibrations, and I love my new looking glass shattered reality."

I look in the mirror to find the stability-healing hero inside. This was taken at the Phoenix Arizona library where I spent a lot of time working on this diary.

In the mirror I caught the site of my reflection. I saw compassion in my heart and alchemically distilled out ancient slime from my current and past life wounds. I did the honest courageous work to heal and forgive ancestral light. Tangled umbilical cords were unraveled. In the gore of human anger I barely clung to the sheer wet cliffs of despair. I lost my hold.

All the while the distance between anger and compassion grew. The heaven of compassion transcends. My Human Compassion hears the billions of voices now heard 3 = ॐ sound vibrations of eons of unheard and heard souls.

In the blood of anger lay the compassionate unions of woman and man. Unite all backgrounds, all castes, all heroes, all flaws, all women, all men, all transgender, and all humanity light of our oneness-tribe. I am one vote of billions to say enough is enough. It is www.pokethedog.net where positive changes begin.

I had spent the last three years trying just the right cover for this diary. I was at the post office in west end Atlanta Georgia. I had a feeling when I mailed a crystal ball (Hyper-Love Forgiven had given me) back to her, something good would come.

While standing in line a random person behind me said, "Do you believe in pay it forward?" I whole-heartedly said, "I have been doing pay it forward my entire life." She gave me the stamps that are on the cover of this diary.

I went to mail the package a lady at the counter said, "Is this package fragile?" "I said yes" I looked down at the package and realized this is my cover. Humanity owns justice, liberty, freedom, and equality forever!

How does Pay it forward and Poke The Dog heal?

We succeed through stirring our soul and what's our passion. We open doors and turn imagination into action. We create new ways to heal humanity through shared Pangaea compassions. We bridge Pangaea healing communities together.

Stability-Healing Questions

What does the number three remind MHC of?

What healing does MHC see in any light source?

What is MHC trying to do with pay it forward?

What does MHC find hopeful about the healer vision?

What shelters does MHC need to create?

What are the MHC occupy movement word of 201 ॐ ?

Why is MHC nimble tribal type government important to own?

Who does MHC say is responsible for cleaning our streets?

What does MHC say about improving our news agencies?

What does MHC say about healing veteran stability heroes?

What does MHC say about healing sensory stability heroes?

How does MHC prove most of humanity is to be trusted?

How does MHC prove most of humanity owns compassion?

What does MHC say about poke the dog healing?

Transcending Light Pictures

I took a picture of AStringOfWords while walking across the street from Madison Square Gardens in New York City. I was shocked to see my name "Dan" in lights! The odds that I would catch my name randomly in this string of words is impossible! This picture is one of many things on my transcending light quest that have me completely believe that Angels are helping my journey.

Can you remember a childhood job you needed in your adult year?

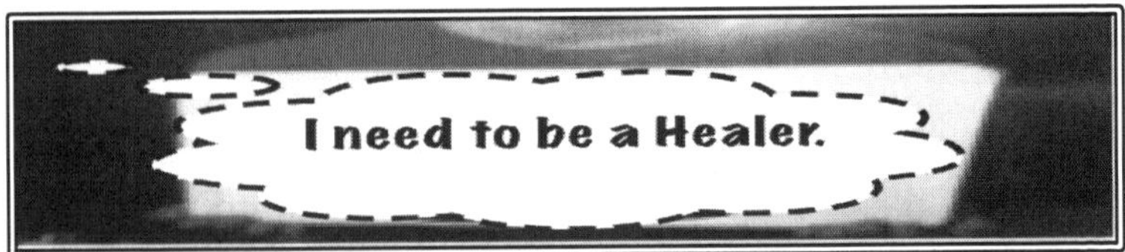

How can you get your inner-self child dream job?

Taking out the trash of others is a symbol of compassion. This is a picture of my shadow aura over trashcans. MHC needs to hear veteran and sensory stability hero stories.

A major influence on my life has been my step-sister Carole. She has been in a wheel chair since her teenage years. She helped get the American's with Disabilities Act (ADA) passed. The ADA improved sensory stability hero rights and rids discrimination. Many institutions had to remodel major sections of their buildings interior and exterior to allow wheelchair accessibility Sensory stability heroes own greater freedom and independence to accessing public and private facilities. Parking spots, elevators, buses, and bathrooms were improved to help our heroes. Not everything is perfect about the ADA. We still need to maintain vigilance to ensure that places accommodate heroes.

Carole travels the world to test wheelchair accessibility in other countries. Many of these countries rate poorly because they do not have an ADA. We must push the United Nations to make ADA compliance for all of Pangaea.

I came up with some ideas for this diary by watching her social activism and her need to make "life fairer". I am grateful to have a life filled with influential and successful women.

Veteran stability heroes pay the highest price so we own freedom. What compassion-based pay it forward help can we give veterans?

Some major challenges humanity faces are poverty, pollution, famine, and war. Some solutions are compassion-based healing, medications, nutrition, and education.

What is freedom?

We have freedom of speech but fewer and fewer voice now heard words are spoken. We have freedom of thought with no one pushing humanity towards creative thinking.

My shadow aura is in a sundial at the Phoenix Arizona Botanical Gardens. Our transcending light vibrations are helping me point the next direction in my life! I am to hike in beautiful Northern Arizona.

I read library stories of compassion for overcoming. This picture was taken at the Denver Colorado Library where I worked on this diary.

I am on a life-long transcending light quest to gather information on how to own stability. Every day I must decide what is best for owning needs. I must save and also eat nutritious meals.

Between eating well and saving I choose both.

I am my own unique inner-self team temple priest. I enter my inner-self home temple. I took this picture at a Hindu Temple in Atlanta, Georgia.

We meet at a "Legacy Table" to discuss equal human civil rights, equally distributed economics, and how to heal all Pangaea humanity.

Stability prevents an early death, divorce, and or bankruptcy.

My vows are my legend to own an inner-self transcending journey.

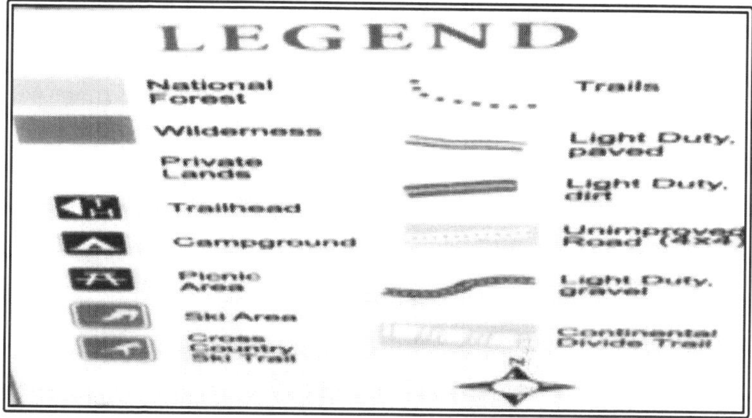

We work to allow all humanity to own nutritious food in their bellies.

Without nutritious food in the belly it is impossible to be educated, own needs, and own safety, acceptance, and stability. Nutritious food is the vital foundation to owning healed. I work with humanity to own healing inner-self homes, careers, learning, influence, and support for those in need.

What is the valuable information MHC learns while on a transcending light quest? Think of the visual and writing discoveries made. Could MHC have found these alone? How much can we know about the over seven billion inhabitants on earth? Is it reasonable for MHC to fear the journey humanity is on? What does MHC want for humanity, which is not happening?

Sometimes people choose others for all the wrong reasons. How does this relate to negative ancestral inheritance? How does it help to carefully think about why you are in a certain relationship, which might own abuse or self-abuse?

The following is a picture of a paperweight I took while visiting Phoenix, Arizona. This is my symbol of our divine transcending light vibrations. It shows its unique blends of light that are in everyone and everything.

Thank you for your honest courageous work to heal!

I look forward to visit with you and compassion-based listen to your inner-self love, inner-self playful, voice now heard, inner-self woman, inner-self man, inner-self forgiven, others-self forgiven, my human compassion, inner-self protected, voice now validated, compassion-based parent, inner-self transcending, and entire inner-self team!

This is the site in Tucson Arizona of the January 8, 2011 Congresswoman Gifford tragedy. Humanity shall never forget. transcending light vibrations and humanity heals us beyond chaos.

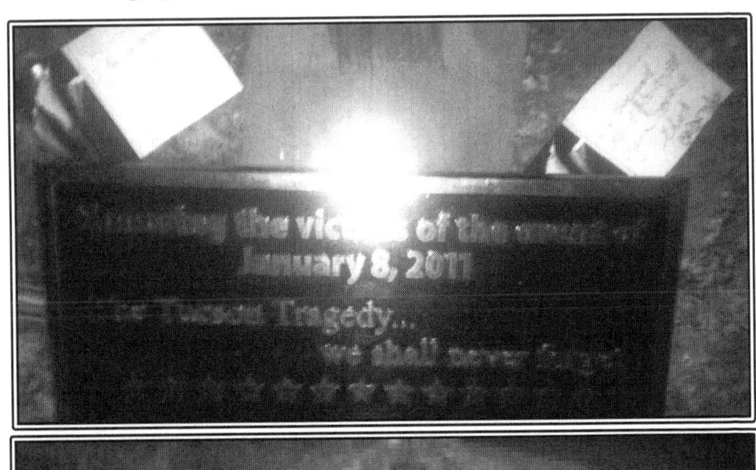

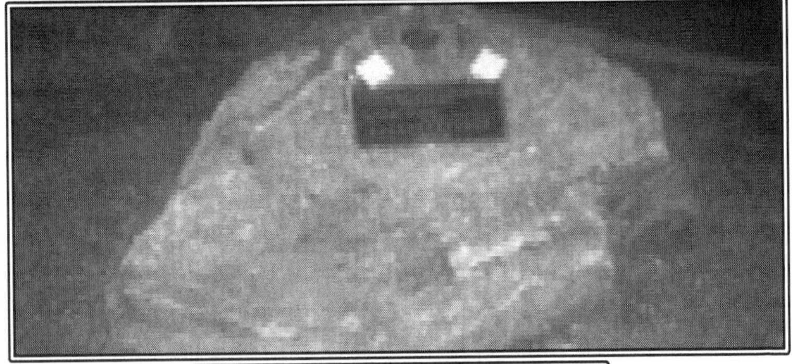

I stabilize, attach, and transform my unique transcending journey. I can obtain this three by owning inner-self love, love of transcending light vibrations Tuns, and compassion.

Stabilize-Attach-Transform

When in love, I learned to own unconditional love disciplined.

Find anyone that's hiked major portions of a trail, fought in a war against extremists, owned struggle to get out of bed, or is turned away from a job because they are in a wheel chair. This is the person I need to hire!

Inner-self prayer Flags are hung for the wind to carry humanity and the earth AUM sound vibrations across transcending light vibrations. They own happiness, prosperity, protection, enlightenment, and overcoming natural disasters. They encourage compassion, thankfulness, fearlessness, and responsibility. Balancing our inner-self team owns stability for our well-being. These symbols balance humanity and transcending light vibrations yin yang elements of earth, water, fire, air, and space. This is a picture of my roommate's door while staying in Forest Hills New York City. The second picture is the Garchen institute in Prescott Arizona where I slept in a Stupa for five nights. These were healing experiences!

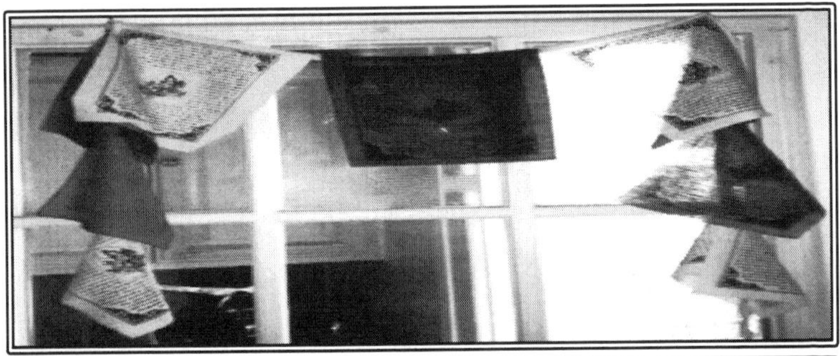

The earth and humanity always need balancing. Our inner-self prayer flags move in the AUM wind sound vibrations to own transcending light vibrational healing. The transcending AUM vibrations protect humanity from harm. It brings harmony to each and every AUM umbilical cord.

I used to view cities through a looking glass prison. I own stability to survive in the city. This is a picture of Manhattan New York City through a cage in Brooklyn New York City.

Everything I had once relied on vanished.
I viewed our cities through prison bars.
I went on a transcending light quest without knowing my future.

Where was i going and why?
What was I going to do or not do?

I hiked in a sky so clear all our stars are so bright!
I start floating from the ground.
I slipped into the unknown.
I am drawn into transcending light vibrations pulling me in.

Would I fall in love or fall out?
Would I fall into stability or instability?
I look up at the tallest buildings.

I climb the highest mountains.
Everyone is healing!

The deeper I hike in the dark forest the more fear I owned.
The farther I hiked on lonely city streets the more fear I owned.

The streets and trails are paved with realities.
I embrace our transcending light vibrations.

The eight hundred pound gorilla became a stuffed toy.
Dance, laughter, singing, play, and nature soothe my soul.
The rhythm vibrations calm my AUM umbilical cord.

The media tries to convince me humanity is to be feared.
The news tries to say all humanity owns anger.
I found the truth - humanity owns compassion.

External influences are working hard at keeping me trapped and forever living inside an inner-self prison. I can get hurt in a prison. At the end of the day everyone is trying to feed his or her family. Well our family, my family, and their family are all a team of:

Humanity!

Looking Glass Shattered Song

My looking glass life.
Do I own crisis or chaos?
It's all up to me.

Ya de da de doo da dee
Fa la to la dee

I can own a looking glass shattered life.
Turned away from despair.
I am not yet ready for a toe tag.

Do dee da do do da
Ah ah ah eh ewe

The one I save is I.
As I love my own inner-self team.
Inner-self love defines transcending.

Eh eh eh ee do dah dee

It is inner-self team love.
I forever own stability.
Owning stable-senses tools!

No more shame, blame, or guilt
Inner-self home owned

Eh eh eh ee do dah dee

I look in the mirror.
There is a stability-healing hero looking back.

Do dee da do do da
Ah ah ah eh ewe

Healing Rain Song

Owning a unique inner-self home.
Shared transcending light vibrations.
Healing rain is here.
Wash away my shame.

Wash away my anger.
Wash away my suffering.
Owning the healing rains of inner-self love.

Ewwww ya ya ya wah wah do we dah.

How does my inner-self team shine?
Everyone is stable.
Everyone is safe.

How does my inner-self light shine to ancestors?
Healing rain is here.
It washes away delusions and exaggerations.

Ewwww ya ya ya wah wah do we dah.

Wash away my guilt.
Wash away my fear.
Wash away my fantasy.

I own positive actions.
Uncovering my compassion-based parent.

Oh yay ya ya.

I support life is transcending heroes

Ewwww ya ya ya wah wah do we da.

Neutral clear enlightened compassion filled journey.
Inner-Self love is owned by all humanity.

These diary tools own my healed unique transcending journey.

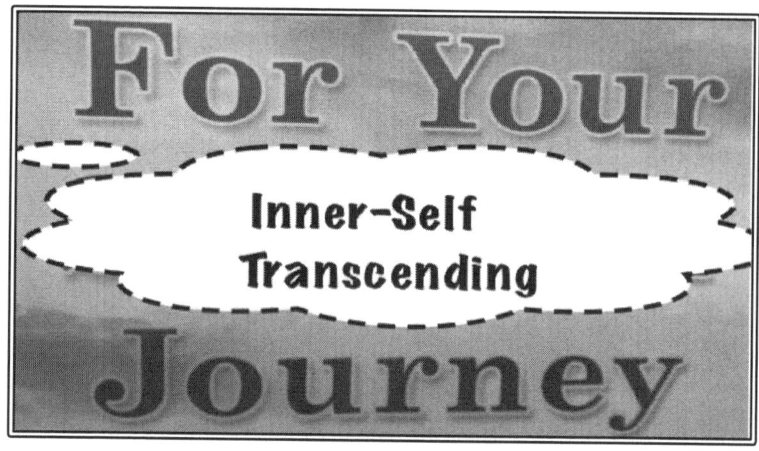

My inner-self team wrote *Looking Glass Shattered* to serve you.

Written by: Inner-Self Love
Written by: Inner-Self Playful
Written by: Voice Now Heard
Written by: Inner-Self Woman
Written by: Inner-Self Man
Written by: Inner-Self Forgiven
Written by: Others-Self Forgiven
Written by: My Human Compassion
Written by: Inner-Self Protected
Written by: Voice Now Validated
Written by: Compassion-Based Parent
Written by: Inner-Self Transcending

We look forward
to serving you!

This photo was taken at a Take Back The Night Foundation event in downtown Phoenix Arizona. This foundation creates safe communities and respectful relationships through awareness events and initiatives. Ending sexual assault, domestic violence, dating violence, sexual abuse and all sexual violence.

TIP Δ – Energy healing helps our inner-self light bulb glow to "on" during our lives. Reiki is one of many approaches to energy healing. Through healer hands transcending light vibrations flows through another, helping them own inner-self love and own our transcending light vibrations love. If one's inner-self light bulb energy is dim or off, then we are more likely to get ill, and if it is on, we are more capable of health, happiness, and success.

I am on an all 3-transcending taxi in Denver, Colorado.

This is a view of downtown St. Louis from the downtown arch. A friend of mine and I stopped here on our road trip to Colorado.

Constant streaming technology overloads makes it difficult for anyone to attach with third-eye transcending all around us.

Pay it forward and www.pokethedog.net stays attached with new neighborhood events.

What's New In The Neighborhood?

Everyone is reincarnated from millions of past lives. In a past life everyone has been of every country, every gender, transgender, race, rich, poor, every ethnicity, every caste, every sexual orientation, every religion, every senses limitation, and every national origin.

TIP Δ – Everyone bully who dominated me, hurt me, rejected me, abused me, and gave me harm is actually someone in a past life I did the same thing to. This defines Karma.

TIP Δ – In a past life it was my Father - Abusive Father Forgiven – who I controlled. In a past life it was my Mother – Angry Mother Forgiven who I was angry at. In a past life it was my bullies who I did the bullying to.

TIP Δ – The two statements above are the best healing advice I give.

TIP Δ – Another healing is for me to own inner-self loved and then holding this same love for transcending light vibrations.

I do whatever it takes to own inner-self love, whatever healing tools I own, and whatever healing education I can get. I hold this dearly into my chakras and into my transcending light vibrational breathing. I will reach the point in my life where every second, every minute, and every hour hold inner-self love.

I let my inner-self chatter fade away and become one with my third-eye, heart, body, and all chakras attachments with transcending light vibrational energy, love, and light.

I become one of the millions across Pangaea who are now becoming transcended, enlightened, and awakened. We live in amazing times. Everyone is in a unique process of transcending and working through old wounds from this life, all past lifetimes, and all dimensions. Healing sweeps across every city, wilderness, and ocean.

These are not end of days. These are times of the feminine earth healing everything. On December 21, 2012 feminine energy spreads it's healing into humanity, Pangaea, and us. Each of us has are in the Age of Aquarius. Each of us will own a voice now validated. I will be your voice now validated in 201 ॐ and beyond.

I took my lost existence to new life illuminating transformations. Am I neglecting myself?

The empty void deep within my inner-self child cries to be voice now heard so my inner-self parent owns a voice now validated. I forgave my old wounds weighing heavily upon my heart. I rediscover myself through personal transcending transformations.

I own a reality every human shall own equal human civil rights. No matter what someone did or where someone has been it is never to late to change a unique transcending journey.

When I spoke of old wounds it was a story of being lost without hope and faith. My life does not need to be like that.

I listen carefully to myself asking myself and writing in my diary so I may own inner-self love returning me to my womb-healed days. I will be a stability-healing hero. I could never have survived my transcending light quest without the help of humanity and transcending light vibrations. I will help heal humanity.

My Human Compassion is here to offer 3-compassion-based help. I don't believe in giving away the fish or handouts. I believe in teaching how to fish. At what age did this person retreat from womb-healed? Was it twelve? Twenty-seven? Fifty-three?

I vote yes on 119-fearlessness in 201  and beyond!

I need change and change will occur. I replace negative action with positive. I set realistic healing goals. I relax and cope with anxiety and stress. I own differences of opinions and arguments yet I own compassion-based listening and well-being availability. I rely on 3 compassion-based healing. I share my faith in humanity.

Change has felt threatening to me. I felt I was losing things of great value. This is a necessary change I must go through. It owns letting go of the old and owning the new.

TIP Δ – I let go of old ways of schooling children, old legal methods, and any other old methods not keeping up with the new Age of Aquarius. I let go of all ancient systems and transcend into new healthy ways of living. Old ways are being replaced with new. We are fortunate to live in a time of great change. People might think it is end-of-days but it is not. Out with the old and in with the new. I work with humanity in bringing healthy healing changes.

TIP Δ – The term cognitive conflict is when I used to believe in old systems and now I let new healthier beliefs in. An inconsistency in beliefs and behaviors are something I change in order to eliminate inner-self conflict. My once blind following of old systems get looking glass shattered through my human compassion.

Do not give up. You have stability healing heroes, transcending light vibrations, and my human compassion to help you. You always have us. When it seems that all is rough. You can fall back on us. Hold your inner-self transcending accepting whatever may come or may go. Loving transcending light vibrations flow through us all.

Accepting my brand new beliefs owns awareness of new life truths. When all around Pangaea might on the surface appear to be getting worse remember transcending light vibrations shines bright upon us. My Human Compassion is right there with you as your reading these words.

It is time to breath in the love of inner-self team presence. Each of us is loved. I see your beauty, talent, and grace. Where will my next transcending light quest take me?

Asia, Africa, or Europe?

Transcending stage one, transcending stage two, and transcending stage three refer to any personal transformations a person might go through (i.e. butterfly to caterpillar).

Transcending stage one is when I rise up from despair and own looking glass shattered. The lower vibrations of my energy are cleared as I move from transcending stage one to stage two. Transcending stage two clears old wounds. I no longer live in the past. I am womb-healed. The *Looking Glass Shattered* diary details my transcending stage one and some stage two transformations. My future diaries focus on stage two and stage three transformations.

The transcending stage three is fully embracing transcending light vibrations of inner-self love and compassion. I let transcending into my personality for greater purposes and renewed energies for living. My transcending stage three allows me to transform into a completely different person. I move from caterpillar to butterfly.

My next diary has me traveling through India and many other world countries to compile things we have discovered at healing old wounds at community, state, country, and Pangaea transcending's. I need to meet as many of the over seven billion of you I can.

I want to help implement programs were women Chief Executive Officers (CEO) meets with women of countries actively oppressing women and forcing them into being objects to be owned. These women leaders bring hope, overcoming, and new reality to other women. These types of programs give rise to the earth feminine so we can save humanity.

I am running for President of the USA in 2016 under my new political party called the "compassion party". Vote compassion in 2016 and beyond!

I gained information and new friends in San Diego, California.

TIP Δ – Each of us needs to be validated on our unique transcending journey. This is at the train station going from Santa Ana, California to San Diego, California.

Let's stay cord attached and learn more about MHC and 333.

Facebook Author Fan Page: Looking Glass Shattered
Facebook Friend Page: MHC Comp
Goodreads: My Human Compassion
Twitter: @myhumancompass